'TIS the SEASON to FEEL INADEQUATE

**Holidays, Special Occasions and Other
Times Our Celebrations Get Out of Hand**

*Thanks for you interest!
Hope you enjoy.*

DOROTHY ROSBY

'Tis the Season to Feel Inadequate: Holidays,
Special Occasions and Other Times Our
Celebrations Get Out of Hand
Published by Unhinged Press
Rapid City, SD

ISBN: 978-0-578-29552-7
HUMOR / Essays

Cover and interior design by Victoria Wolf,
wolfdesignandmarketing.com. Copyright belongs to author.

QUANTITY PURCHASES: Professional groups, clubs, and
other organizations may qualify for special terms when
ordering quantities of this title. For information, visit
www.dorothyrosby.com/contact.

For my great big, wonderful family in honor of the many holidays we've shared over the years. It's a shame turkeys don't have more drumsticks.

Contents

New Year's

Valentine's Day

SPRING

The Christmas Letter to Make You Feel Better About Yourself

Merry Christmas friends!

I bet you're surprised to be getting a Christmas letter from me. I know I'm surprised you're getting a Christmas letter from me, especially before Christmas. But seeing how people who get their holiday letters out early get more letters in return, I thought I'd join the ranks of the organized this year. I would have sent this in June if I thought it would get me more gifts.

Besides, I have a lot of news to share this year. For one thing, I finally finished writing this book I've been working on for about twenty-five years. It's all about holidays and the way they bring out the worst in us. And I start with Christmas and work my way through the year because no holiday makes us feel more inadequate than Christmas, except maybe Nude Recreation Week. But I don't really cover that one in this book.

Much of the damage our self-esteem suffers at Christmas is caused by…well… Christmas letters. That's why I don't always send them. I care about other people's feelings.

I'm sure you've gotten those letters where the writer carries on about the exciting adventures and numerous successes their family has had over the past year, leaving you feeling jealous, inferior and as interesting as a tree sloth. This won't be one of those. In fact, you should be feeling pretty good about yourself by the time I'm finished.

It was actually kind of a tough year for me. For one thing, I had a preview of how you'll spend all eternity if you die and go to hell. I didn't actually keep track, but I'm sure I was on hold for approximately three full days back in March. I'm not normally a patient person, but I was encouraged to persist by the elevator version of Eric Clapton's "You Look Wonderful Tonight," which was repeated at least 175 times. That and the message reminding me that "all calls are answered in the order they're received, so hanging up only means you'll have to wait all over again later."

Then I had a little lip balm emergency this summer. You probably didn't know it was possible to have an emergency involving lip balm. Me neither. But one day when I was digging for mine, I heard a voice from the depths of my purse saying, "Nine one one. What's your emergency?" I had accidentally dialed 911 on my cellphone, which is amazing considering the chaos at the bottom of my purse. I doubt I could do as well in an actual emergency. I hung up fast because that seemed wiser than saying, "I lost my lip balm."

Actually, a lot of my problems this year can be blamed on technology, though that was the only one I can blame on lip balm. My printer died, my computer crashed and I had email troubles. If you emailed me last summer and didn't hear back right away, that's why. Either that or I was mad at you.

At one point, I was under my desk with the telephone jammed between my ear and my shoulder. "Now make sure it's plugged in," the tech person said, a little patronizingly I thought. I wanted to yell, "Why wouldn't it be plugged in? I'm underneath a desk tangled up in cables and cords? Who in their right mind would have crawled under here to unplug it?" I didn't though because the call was being monitored for quality assurance purposes.

If that's not bad enough, I also had some minor health issues, proving that old saying that if ain't one thing, it's two others. In fact, I started this year out on the couch with my feet up. You may wonder how that's different from any other year. Well, this time I had a good excuse. I had foot surgery and had to quit walking for a few weeks. Incidentally, in September I had to quit walking again because I lost my fitness tracker.

The surgery wasn't a big deal. I just had a bone spur removed from the tip of my big toe. As you can imagine, this is an inconvenient place for a bone spur and I'll tell you what else is inconvenient: trying to get in out of a bathtub on one foot so you don't get your bandages wet. Save a toe; break a leg.

I also had a bad case of tennis elbow. I'd tell you that's why my handwriting is unreadable but I hate to lie during the holiday season. The funny thing is, I can't even remember the last time I played tennis. I think they call it tennis elbow because that's easier to pronounce than "lateral epicondylitis," its official name. Plus, it sounds more interesting than "inflammation of the elbow tendons" and more glamorous than "washing the windows elbow" or "chopping vegetables elbow." According to my health consultant, Google, any activity that involves repetitive use of the forearm can lead to tennis elbow. That's why plumbers, painters and cooks are all candidates for it, and it explains why I'll be avoiding plumbing, painting and cooking from here on out.

And here's another reason to avoid cooking. Our dishwasher isn't working right so if you're wondering what to get me for Christmas, I could really use a new one. Using ours these days is a lot like having a couple of kids do the dishes. There's a lot of noise coming from the kitchen but nothing is really getting clean.

For about twelve seconds I thought about not replacing it. We're empty nesters. How many dishes can we dirty? As it turns out, a lot. You don't realize how many dirty dishes you're personally responsible for until you have no dishwasher to wash them and no child at home to blame them on. We'll definitely be replacing the dishwasher, just in case washing dishes causes tennis elbow.

On a more positive note, I celebrated National Root Beer Float Day on August 6. But because I'm not particularly fond of root beer, I had chocolate syrup on my ice cream instead of root beer. I enjoyed it so much that I've decided to celebrate it again next year. I may not wait until August though, because truly, National Root Beer Float Day was the highlight of my year. Do you feel better about yourself yet?

Inadequately yours,

Dorothy Rosby

P.S. Portions of a few of the essays in this book have appeared in one of my other collections. They were just that good. Also I'm lazy.

Lie—and Other Tips for Writing the Perfect Christmas Letter

WHEN I WAS GROWING UP, my father strung all the Christmas cards my family received in a big X across the ceiling in our living room. I don't receive enough Christmas cards to make an X on my ceiling. I probably couldn't even make a Y or an I. I might be able to make a semicolon.

I used to get more cards, maybe because I used to write more cards. And yes, I mean handwrite. Here's how I did it: I'd start with the first person in my address book, my friend Sue Allen. I'd write out her card then painstakingly copy its contents to my card for the Barbers. Then I'd use the Barbers' card as a model for the Belmonts and so on. I wrote out my cards in much the same way things were done before the invention of the printing press. My handwriting got worse with each card but my stories probably got better.

It was tedious and time-consuming. In fact, the year I sent my last batch of handwritten Christmas cards, everyone from the Johnsons to the Zieglers didn't get them until St. Patrick's Day. But it was so easy I hardly had to think about it. Or anyway, I hardly did think about it. That may explain why over the years several friends complained that they'd received someone else's card. Someone named Sue.

The year Sue got someone else's card I decided to quit sending cards. And I didn't for years. Unfortunately, in return I got fewer and fewer Christmas cards myself until I was down to two—one from my insurance agent and one from a company that sells prepaid funeral plans.

That's when I decided to try a Christmas newsletter. And since then I've started to hear from people I haven't heard from in years. Of course, they're not sending cards; they're sending letters. And those just don't look good strung across my ceiling. Still, I appreciate them.

I also learn from them. As you can see from the actual letters I've included in this book, I do try to heed the most common complaints about holiday letters. If you decide to write one yourself, follow my guidelines:

1. Don't wait. The earlier you get your letter out the more you can enjoy the holiday season. At least that's what I've heard.

2. Embellish. If your life is like mine, your Christmas newsletter could be—how can I say this diplomatically—dull enough to induce coma. I'm not admitting to anything here, but a lot of people think Christmas letters can be honest or they can be interesting.

Still, you'll want to balance the need to embellish with consideration of your readers' feelings of inadequacy. Sure, write glowingly about your many travel adventures but then mention your credit card bills. And be sure and tell them if you lost your luggage, your passport or your temper.

Along with writing about all your successes, tell them about the speeding tickets and overdraft notices you've received during the past year. If you lost anything in the stock market recently, now would be a good time to mention it. Also, legal issues are always interesting.

3. Be brief. A holiday letter should be the trailer, not the whole movie. Don't overdo it when describing the many accomplishments of your children and pets. Avoid blow-by-blow accounts of remodeling projects. And leave out the details of minor and elective surgeries—unless there were complications. Write more than one page and your letter will look like work to read. Your readers may set it aside with the intention of getting to it after the busy holiday season is over. But then it could get tossed out with the wrapping paper and they'll never know about your legal troubles.

4. Include a family photo. A picture really is worth a thousand words—and given the choice I think most people would choose the picture. Besides, a photograph can say a lot that those on your Christmas list would enjoy hearing: You're alive and well. You appear to be happy. And you've gained weight just like they have.

5. Personalize your letter. If you aren't careful your Christmas letter will be about as intimate as the back of a cereal box. But you can easily individualize it by typing the phrase "Merry Christmas" on the salutation line and then handwriting the first name of your recipient beside it, preferably in their favorite color. If you still don't feel your letter is personal enough try enclosing a lock of your hair or your child's tooth.

6. Introduce. If you feel the need to discuss people not all of your readers know, make it a point to explain who they are. For example, "We went to Bill and Ann's for Thanksgiving," should be expanded to "Bill is Nick's cousin who moved here from Phoenix after he met Ann on the internet. Nick is our next-door neighbor who is married to Ann's sister Arlene who worked with me at the first job I had when we moved here in 2017." You get the point—if you made it this far.

7. And finally, keep your wits about you. Never put on a little Christmas music and curl up by your Christmas tree with a cup of cocoa while you write your letter. This is no time to be overcome with Christmas spirit. If you're not careful you may say something to everyone on your address list that you only mean for a few of them. Something like, "If you're ever in town, you're welcome to stay with us."

How to Choose the Perfect Gift or Get Out of Giving One Altogether

'TIS THE SEASON to run up our credit card bills and give our friends and family good head starts on their next garage sale. It doesn't have to be that way. The year I bought two talking trout and a fruit cake at 4 p.m. on Christmas Eve, I decided it was time to change my gift-giving ways. As a public service I'm going to share with you my new rules for gift giving:

When to shop:
- Don't wait until the night before Christmas when all through the house, not a gift has been bought, not even for your spouse. More worthless gadgets, doohickies and thingamabobs are purchased just before Christmas than at any other time of the year. And most of them are bought in those last frantic

moments before the reindeer appear. Shoppers who started out with high hopes break down on December 24 and settle for an electric carrot peeler—or a talking trout.

- But don't buy your gifts too far in advance either. You could forget you bought them—or where you put them. You could accidentally sell them at a garage sale. Or you could find that by Christmas you're not even on speaking terms with the potential recipients, let alone gift-giving terms.

Where to shop and where not to shop:
- Never shop for Christmas gifts on television infomercials. The promise that if you buy one dumb thing, you'll get another dumb thing free is not necessarily a sign of quality. Also, if the infomercial claims the item is not sold in stores keep in mind there might be a really good reason why this is so.
- Avoid shopping online. There's no guarantee that what you see on the screen is what you'll get in the mail. Do an internet search of online shopping scams and you can see a stylish jumpsuit that looked more like pink surgical scrubs when the buyer received it, and an attractive three-piece bedding set that was only one pillowcase when it arrived—and not an attractive one. Your recipient may not appreciate these.
- Shop locally. It's good for your community. When my son was young I spent many hours watching Little League baseball games and I never once saw the name Amazon, Wayfair or Overstock.com

emblazoned on the back of a uniform. Doing business with the good people who are regularly hit up for all manner of donations and sponsorships seems like the least we can do. Anyway, it's easier to return a gift you bought locally and your recipient may want to do that, especially if you got them pink surgical scrubs.

How to maintain your Christmas spirit as you shop:

- Before you leave home, before you spend two hours filling a shopping cart to the brim, before you wait in line for twenty minutes, and before you unload thirteen Christmas gifts, two bottles of shampoo, a bag of Doritos and a case of toilet paper at the check-out, make absolutely certain that you have your wallet. I know from experience that the peace and goodwill everyone feels during this joyful time of year doesn't extend to someone holding up the line at Stuff-Ko.

- Have more than one idea for each person on your gift list. Coming to blows with another shopper over the last sixteen-piece Speed Lock Cordless Drill has a way of dampening the old Christmas spirit. So does calling home from jail.

How to ensure your loved one will appreciate your gift:

- Think long and hard before buying a loved one a personal care item like a tube of cellulite reduction cream or a snore stopper. But if after careful consideration you still think it's a good gift idea, write "from Santa" on the tag.

- If you're tempted to buy a clothing item that looks so perfect for someone on your gift list that you can practically see them in it, consider the possibility that it looks so perfect for them because they already have it.
- Before you purchase a particular gadget or thingamabob for some unsuspecting individual on your Christmas list, ask yourself if they'll use it often enough to keep it within reach. Or will they store it away until that annual or semi-annual occasion when they want to use it but are unable to find it behind their home snow cone machine and their frittata flipper?
- Whatever you choose, be sure to include a gift receipt when you wrap it up. Your recipient will appreciate it and you'll never have to know that they returned the fake tattoo sleeves you bought them.

How to get out of shopping altogether:
- Give gift cards. If you hate to shop, your recipient does it for you and still feels like you're doing them a favor.
- Consider re-gifting. It's thrifty, earth-friendly and only a little tacky. But be careful. I once received a gift-wrapped cheese board with two tags on it: one to me and one to Joyce and David. I'm not Joyce—or David. And I don't need a cheese board, so I gave it to Bill and Karen. I removed the other tags first—I think.
- Make your gifts. Homemade gifts can be very

meaningful. Unfortunately, how meaningful depends entirely on whose home they were made in. If like me, you're not the crafty sort, you'll want to stick to buying gifts—or gift cards. While it truly is better to give than to receive, that's not what you want anyone thinking when they open your gift.

Please Put Me Back on Your Christmas Card List

Hello there! Remember me?

I always figured everyone assumed no news is good news. Unfortunately, I've discovered that if some people don't hear from you for a few years they take you off their Christmas card list. So, in an effort to get back in your good graces and back on your Christmas card list, I'm sending my Christmas letter for this year—and possibly next year as well.

I hope the year was a good one for you. Mine began in a courtroom, which I think you'd agree, is no way to start a new year, especially if you're the defendant. Fortunately I wasn't. It was still stressful though. I was already running late when I arrived at the courthouse for jury duty on January 4, and then my necklace set off the alarm on the metal detector. By the time I got to my seat I was in no mood to be fair and impartial. In the end, I wasn't selected to be on the jury anyway. Maybe that's why.

In July we moved our office to our guest room, our guest room to my son's bedroom and my son's bedroom to our office. We had a really good reason for doing this, but for the life of me, right now I can't think what it was. Actually, about halfway through the process I couldn't think what it was. At the time I nicknamed the ordeal the Great Order Restoration Project, but now I see that was naive and overly optimistic since order has yet to be restored.

My cellphone died this year. The good news is all it took was a factory reset to revive it. The bad news is the factory reset locked it. In other words, for several days my phone thought I was a thief trying to break into it. This is the world we live in. Hackers can break into giant corporations and steal all our financial data but we can't get into our own cellphones.

Fortunately, I was able to unlock it after an hour and a half talking on a borrowed landline to an Apple representative. *Unfortunately*, until I got everything reloaded, my cellphone couldn't do a thing except make and receive phone calls. And yes, I realize there was a time when that would have been enough.

After all that, we still felt optimistic enough to buy a harness and leash for our cat. It seems insane now. The cat thinks so too.

Before you judge us you should know that I have several friends who regularly take their cats for walks. Plus there are hundreds of YouTube videos of people who've successfully leash-trained their cats. There are also hundreds of YouTube videos of people who've failed to leash-train their cats. We ignored those.

It turns out that putting our cat in the harness was a little like dressing a greased toddler. And when we finally had him in it, he sank to the ground looking embarrassed and uncomfortable and crawled under the bed as fast as he could go. I'm hopeful about many things in the coming year but taking our cat for a walk isn't one of them.

My husband and I celebrated our anniversary with an Alaskan cruise. We had a glorious time and I hope we don't have to be married for another thirty years before we get to go on another vacation like that one. I will say, a cruise ship is more luxury than we're used to. It's a rare thing for me to eat in a place where you have to dress for dinner, though I do always have something on.

Our steward left chocolate on our pillows every evening too. You don't see that everywhere. But it's not as special as you'd think. It's only one little piece—actually two, one for each of us, but my husband doesn't know that. And why on the pillow? By the time I found it I'd already brushed my teeth.

We did a lot of camping this summer, or as I like to call it, weather modification. Our camping trips are more efficient at causing precipitation than a cloud seeding program, which is why last summer we gave up our tent and built ourselves an ark. I'm joking. Actually we bought a camper, which was easier.

We also did a bit of canoeing. This presents a challenge for me because it means assisting my husband to lift our seventeen-foot aluminum canoe off the top of our vehicle, and I'm not as strong as I look. Fortunately, after so many years of marriage we're a good team. Working together, we've developed a very efficient system that involves lifting the canoe, then flipping it while my husband calls out instructions and I complain about them.

We didn't bring our canoe or drag our camper along with us on our southwest trip this fall. It's cheaper to stay in a camper than it is to stay in a hotel but staying with relatives like we did is cheaper still and it doesn't affect your gas mileage. We took a ton of photos on all of our travels. Hopefully we can get together soon and I'll show you every single one of them on my phone. I know you'll enjoy that.

Your fair and impartial friend,

Dorothy

P.S. Now would you please put me back on your Christmas card list?

A Few Christmas Tunes I'd Like to Roast over an Open Fire

DISCLAIMER: *The opinions expressed in this essay are mine alone. But it is my book so I can do that. You may feel differently. I won't hold it against you.*

I'm fond of Christmas music and I'm sincerely grateful to those radio stations that play it all day, every day from Thanksgiving until Christmas. I can't help singing along with all my favorites, which I'm sure is as entertaining to the people next to me at stoplights as it is annoying to those in the car with me. I'd never get my tree up and my Christmas shopping done if it weren't for music getting me into the spirit of the season. And sometimes even that doesn't work.

I love "O Holy Night," "Away in a Manger" and "Silver Bells." Every time a snowflake falls I burst into a chorus of "It's Beginning to Look a Lot Like Christmas," even if it falls in April. I like "White Christmas" as much as anyone, as long as I don't have to shovel. And "Winter Wonderland" is one of my favorites. You know it: "Later on we'll perspire, 'cause it's warm by the fire. Plus we're afraid of the plans that we've made, walking in a winter wonderland." It's something like that.

But there are a few Christmas songs that make me grateful Christmas comes but once a year, and "Santa Baby" is at the top of the list. "Do You Hear What I Hear?" (See how I did that? I really like that one.) The singer is flirting with Santa, who, as far as I know, is a happily married man. And all she wants for Christmas is...a lot. Just a fur coat, a convertible, a yacht, a duplex, some checks, a ring, decorations from Tiffany's and the deed to a platinum mine. All I want is to never hear her ask for it all again.

The only wish list longer than hers is in "The Twelve Days of Christmas." I read that it would cost $170,298.03 to buy everything for that twelve-day gift-giving rampage and what would you have to show for it? A noisy mess. Our hapless gift recipient would be forced to sell her gold rings to buy an aviary for all the birds. Then she'd have to put the ladies dancing and the lords-a-leaping to work cleaning it, which would be a real waste of talent.

"All I Want for Christmas Is My Two Front Teeth" is a short but equally annoying Christmas wish song. There's not a child in America who would settle for that. That song should only be performed at elementary school Christmas concerts where it's still cute, even if it is a lie.

"I Saw Mommy Kissing Santa Claus" is another song that should only be sung by small children, and the Chipmunk song, "Christmas Don't Be Late," should only be heard by small children. That song makes me long for a little "Silent Night" which, by the way, is one of my favorites.

And speaking of musical animals, hearing dogs bark "Jingle Bells" is a once-in-a-lifetime experience, by which I mean once in a lifetime is enough. I don't know about chestnuts, but that's one Christmas CD I wouldn't mind roasting over an open fire.

That and "Grandma Got Run Over by a Reindeer." It's mean, it's disrespectful and there's no way it could have happened. Everyone knows reindeer fly.

Finally there's "The Christmas Shoes," a melodramatic song about a boy who goes shoe shopping for his mother while she's home dying. Hear that too many times and you have a hard time believing "It's the Most Wonderful Time of the Year." (Another favorite of mine.)

I'll get through it somehow. I'll sing along with the ones I like and change the station during the ones I don't. December 26 will roll around and I won't have to hear "Last Christmas" and "Baby It's Cold Outside" again for another whole year. "Joy to the World," which I love, by the way.

Merry Christmas from the Envyofall Family

THERE ARE TWO THINGS that make me feel like a boring person. Actually there are more than two, but the ones that come to mind this time of year are writing a Christmas letter and reading everyone else's.

When I write a letter I come to the painful realization that the year has flown by again, that I've been terribly busy but I haven't done a thing worth mentioning. Worse, when I read all the newsy holiday letters I receive I think the writers must have had more days since last Christmas than I had, and apparently more money, energy and ambition as well.

I don't think I'm alone in my feelings of inadequacy either. Consider the following actual letter I made up. You'll see in brackets what an unfortunate reader might be thinking as she reads this holiday greeting from the Envyofall family.

Merry Christmas from the Envyofalls!

We hope your year was as wonderful as ours was! *[I'm pretty sure it wasn't.]* We started the year with a January vacation in Hawaii. *[Now I know it wasn't.]* Since the children are both doing so well in school we decided taking them out for two weeks would be acceptable, and they enjoyed themselves thoroughly. *[I'll bet their teachers did too.]*

In June Maxwell and I celebrated our twentieth anniversary with a month in Italy. *[What a coincidence! My husband and I celebrated our anniversary in June too—at the Olive Garden.]* You can see photos of both vacations on our family website. *[You can see our vacation photos too—if my phone is working.]*

Tad and Tillie are both doing great in school. *[You mentioned that.]* How blessed we are to have such clever, well-behaved children. *[That's not how I remember them.]*

Tillie is a senior. She's a computer whiz and has helped so many people with computer issues that she finally decided to start her own business. She's also a fabulous saxophone player and already has her own band which has won countless competitions. Between the business and the band she's earning lots of money just in time for college. But what do you know! She won a full-ride scholarship to Superior University and won't need any of it. *[She could send it to me.]*

Tad is a straight-A student and president of his class. He just became an Eagle Scout and he's fluent in Chinese, Spanish and French. He's also active in 4-H, football, soccer, basketball, baseball, track, band, choir, debate, theatre, orchestra and dressage. *[That kid never did have an ounce of ambition.]*

In June Maxwell was promoted to Vice President at his company. *[I don't see how. He's never at work.]* And I continue to run a successful import/export business out of our home. It's doing so well that I've been able to fully fund our retirement plan and purchase a winter home in Arizona. I also volunteer around twenty hours a week for the less fortunate. *[I'm less fortunate and you didn't do a thing for me.]*

And last but not least, Snookums won Best of Show at the Kennel Club Dog Show. We love him dearly and are so proud of him! *[Spotty peed on the carpet and bit my mother-in-law. We still love him... most days.]*

Happy holidays to you and yours! We think of you often and hope to see you soon. *[We think of you often too and desperately hope that when we see you next we'll have something to show for ourselves.]*

Sincerely,

The Envyofalls

Peace on Earth and
War at Home

AH, THE HOLIDAY SEASON; a joyous time for families to come together, create new traditions and fight about the old ones. It's not that they're disagreeable people—well, some of them are disagreeable people—it's just that couples bring to their marriages the traditions of the families they grew up in. And they desperately want to pass their customs on to their children. Not only that, they feel that their partner's traditions are—how can I say this diplomatically—silly and stupid and therefore not worth keeping alive.

NOTE: The world's religions are outside the scope of my expertise, as most things are, so for the purposes of this essay I will focus on those couples who agree to celebrate Christmas. But that may be all they agree on.

Let's start with the most basic question: When to decorate? One partner believes that if the Christmas decorations are up more than two weeks out, the true meaning of the holiday season will be forgotten and boredom will set in. They also hope that if they wait long enough they'll get out of decorating altogether.

The other partner thinks that if they're going to go to all the trouble, they ought to enjoy the decorations for as long as possible. Not to mention it's easier to decorate the outside of the house while it's seventy-five degrees. Why not put the decorations up on an unseasonably cool day in July?

The family must also decide between a real and an artificial tree. One partner takes the emotional angle that artificial trees don't smell as nice or look as, well, real. The other side is more logical. "Yes, but artificial trees don't drop needles; they're never flat on one side; and we won't have to chop a lovely, living tree to death every year." Maybe that's a little emotional too.

If the family decides on a real tree, they must choose between buying one and cutting one. "Remember how much fun we had last year tromping through the forest and cutting down our tree?"

"Yes, and remember getting stuck in the snow and losing the chainsaw?"

Wherever they get their tree, some members of the family like pine, some like fir and at least one is still grumbling that an artificial tree would be easier. Finally, in the spirit of the season there are compromises made and pouting all the way home.

Then there's the subject of gifts. One parent panics if the gifts aren't bought and wrapped by August 1. The other holds out hope that Santa will show up rendering shopping unnecessary. When this doesn't happen, and it seldom does, this partner believes there is nothing wrong with shopping on December 24—except that his/her spouse grew up opening gifts on Christmas Eve.

"That makes no sense. Everyone knows Santa only works one night a year."

"If Santa did his job we wouldn't be discussing this. Maybe it's time we tell the kids the truth."

"Not yet! Remember how upset they were when they caught me filling the Easter baskets."

"You weren't filling them! You were eating out of them. Anyway, thinking about Santa keeps them awake."

"Perfect. They'll be alert for midnight services."

"Midnight? They might be alert, but I don't intend to be."

The question of staying home or traveling to share the holiday with relatives can also be divisive, and more so with certain relatives. If the family stays home there's the subject of what to prepare for holiday meals. Ham or prime rib? Turkey or tofu?

If they're traveling they don't have to decide but they do have to eat—or pretend to. And there are good reasons some holiday foods are eaten only once a year. It can take a full year to summon the courage to eat lutefisk, fruit cake or oyster stew again. Personally I could eat oyster stew on any holiday, including the Fourth of July. But I don't think my family would agree to that tradition.

Decorating: A Family Affair

A CERTAIN GUEST ONCE CRITICIZED my husband and me because we didn't have any Christmas decorations up in our home. We pointed out that while there was not a plastic Santa or a wreath or even a Christmas tree in sight, we did have a manger scene on display. We told her that by having a crèche only, we were focusing on the true meaning of Christmas. She, with her emphasis on the trappings of Christmas, was celebrating only the commercial aspects of the holiday. All very true.

It was also true that the manger was the only Christmas decoration we could find. We hadn't yet unpacked all our boxes from our recent move—four years before—and the decorations were somewhere in the depths of our basement where Rudolph himself couldn't have found them.

Eventually our ornaments resurfaced. But we were still in no hurry to begin decorating, in part because we were afraid the above-mentioned guest might visit more often.

Besides, decorating takes time. The holiday season is so busy. Everyone has the same number of hours in a day, and some people like to spend theirs decorating. I like to spend mine on activities that are more meaningful to me, like driving around town looking at other people's Christmas lights.

Things started to change as our son grew older. After all, Christmas is for children—and retailers. One day he asked why there were pretty lights on houses all over town but none on ours. I told him, "As soon as you're old enough to climb a ladder we can have lights on our house." We never have had lights on our house.

At some point we began decorating inside our home, however, and none too successfully. My husband and I couldn't even agree about what makes a perfect Christmas tree. He didn't enjoy looking for them, but he never trusted me to pick one out alone. The one time I did that I bought the spindliest tree on the lot because I felt sorry for it. "It doesn't care," he said. "It's dead." But I cared.

One year we bought a giant tree. Then we didn't have enough lights for a tree that big, and it turned out, even fewer that worked. We purchased more lights until we had a grand total of 175, which was, according to the package, perfect for a six-foot tree. For taller trees, as ours apparently was, we were instructed to add thirty-five lights for every foot over six. Big deal, I thought. What difference can thirty-five lights make? I'll tell you. They'll cover the bottom of a seven-foot tree, that's what.

Still, it looked okay to people passing by outside our picture window—they couldn't see the bottom. Then one day the top string stopped working. Outside or inside, the middle of our tree was always beautiful.

Despite everything, now and then I catch myself getting excited about decorating our home this year. In my weaker moments I envision a happy family outing as we venture out to choose a tree together. I see us digging through our ornaments—if we can find them—and oohing and aahing over each one. We'll put on some Christmas music, start the fireplace and make hot chocolate. Then we'll spend the afternoon transforming our home into a Christmas showcase.

Then, just before I'm overcome with holiday spirit, I remember the other reason I don't like to decorate. To misuse an old saying, "Decorate and the whole family decorates with you, but you put the decorations away alone."

And I always do—eventually. What goes up must come down, so long after half the population has already given up on their New Year's resolutions I resolve to take down our decorations. It's never nearly as fun as putting them up and the longer I wait the worse it gets. I don't play Christmas music and drink hot cocoa while I work because some years it's July by the time I get around to the job.

Every year I find I either have more ornaments or fewer boxes than I did when we decorated. Plus I have a tangled-up, twenty-foot strand of mini-twinkle lights, half of which don't twinkle anymore. But dealing with them is no way to start a new year, so I toss them in the box in a heap on the off chance that by next year I'll have developed more patience and dexterity.

My husband helps me wrestle our now artificial tree back into its box, which seems to have shrunk. Then he gives directions and I complain about them as we attempt to haul it down two flights of stairs to the basement, quashing any good will we've developed over the holidays.

No Elephants Were Harmed in the Making of this Essay

THERE'S A BIG BOX in my guest room containing one redneck coloring book (never used), four pink flamingos (brand-new), one wrench beer opener (still in the package) and an assortment of other equally useful items. I keep the box there partly because my guest room has become something of a storage unit and partly because I'm hoping one of my guests will steal it from me.

Unfortunately, so far everyone who's stayed with me has been too honest to steal. Or maybe they just have better taste.

It's okay though. I'm about to part with a few things. 'Tis the season for that curious tradition known as the White Elephant Gift Exchange. The term "white elephant" refers to a useless or troublesome possession, which is exactly what one receives during a White Elephant Gift Exchange. No actual elephants are exchanged at these events, which is lucky because my guest room isn't that big.

The exchange goes by various other names including Rob Your Neighbor, Thieving Secret Santa, Grinch Exchange and Yankee Swap. As far as I know no Yankees are swapped either, though I could fit at least a couple of those in my guest room.

The rules vary, but basically each participant supplies one amusing, impractical or downright dumb gift such as a set of muffin-top baking cups, a high-heel tape dispenser or soap in the shape of false teeth. The group determines order, the first victim opens a wrapped gift and turns to the next victim. Every partaker after that chooses a wrapped gift or steals from someone else who's already selected. When someone's gift is stolen, that person can either choose another wrapped gift to open or steal from another player. The game is over when everyone has a useless item to store in their guest room.

Throughout the exchange, those who don't like their gifts, which is almost everyone, try to persuade others to steal it. "This bacon cologne is so you. You know you want it." "Come on! Everyone should have at least one propeller beanie." It's all quite entertaining and I never want to do it again.

I've had the dubious good fortune of attending many White Elephant Gift Exchanges which explains my redneck coloring book, pink flamingos and wrench beer opener. You didn't think I bought those myself, did you?

As someone who's trying to downsize, it goes against everything in me to attend a social event and come home with something I don't need, don't want and can't regift in good conscience. With that in mind, here's my strategy for winning at the White Elephant Gift Exchange game.

1. Before you choose a gift to bring to the party, make absolutely certain that it's a White Elephant Gift Exchange you're going to. You don't want to be the only one who brings fuzzy dice or a thirty-year-old macroeconomics textbook to the party.

2. Never buy a white elephant gift. That's a waste of money and it only encourages manufacturers to make more. Instead, dig through gifts you've been given. Often an item that was not intended to be a white elephant can easily pass for one. Just make sure the person who gave it to you won't be at the party.

3. Once at the party, make every effort to be the last person to choose a gift. Often order is chosen by drawing numbers. That means you'll have to cheat. I'm kidding. But the last person in the White Elephant Gift Exchange does have the advantage because they can choose the least dumb of all the dumb gifts. Still, don't cheat. It's not worth ruining your reputation over. Or maybe it is.

4. Never choose the most beautifully wrapped gift. Fancy wrapping is almost always a ploy by the giver to convince you to choose their A *Christmas Story* leg lamp or the stocking cap with a beard attached.

5. Never choose the largest gift. A large box often holds many smaller boxes, all containing baby elephants. This is usually a sign that the giver is trying to pare down the selection of white elephant gifts in her guest room. Meanwhile, a small gift in an unattractive brown paper bag is often a gift card purchased on the way to the party by someone who nearly forgot about the occasion.

6. If you get a gift you can tolerate, do all you can to discourage others from stealing it. Sneeze on it if you have to.

7. Finally, if you really don't want your gift, and most likely you won't, "forget" it when you leave the party. I was once at a party where all thirty-some guests hid the gifts we'd received throughout our host's home. That included the case of canned sardines I brought to give away. Our lucky host was finding sardines and white elephants until Valentine's Day. The rest of us went home gift-free if not guilt-free. Merry Christmas to us!

Keep Your Partridge; I'll Take a Roast Chicken

I SAW WHERE I COULD ORDER "The Twelve Days of Christmas" as a cellphone ring tone. I didn't though. I don't believe anything would sap my Christmas spirit quite like hearing that song every time someone calls me—except maybe hearing "The Little Drummer Boy" every time someone calls.

The thing that's always bothered me about the "Twelve Days of Christmas," besides that it's repetitive and relentless and it takes twelve days to sing it, is that the giver's choice of gifts is just plain ridiculous. By day three, I'd be yelling, "Will you stop! The birds go or I go!"

I do give the guy credit for shopping though. It can't be easy to find four calling birds and seven swans a-swimming this time of year, let alone catch them and put them in the car.

Also, you could never accuse him of being cheap. As of this writing he'd pay a whopping $170,298.03 for all those gifts. That's according to PNC Financial Services Group, which tracks the cost of the gifts in the "Twelve Days of Christmas" every year so that Christmas shoppers can budget better.

I like to think my true love could make better use of $170,298.03. For starters, I need some new tires. I know tires aren't much of a Christmas gift, but with $170,298.03 I bet he could buy me a really nice sweater too.

I've got some suggestions for saving True Love time and money, and more importantly, giving his lady some gifts she'll enjoy. For starters, while a pear tree might be a practical gift, the ground is too hard to plant one right now. You'd think True Love would know that. Instead of a partridge in a pear tree, why not a fresh fruit basket and a nice roast chicken?

And rather than two turtle doves, how about two Dove bars? The chocolate, not the soap. Soap might send the wrong message.

On day three True Love presents three French hens which, as it turns out, are nothing but chickens with accents. His sweetheart has already had roast chicken three times this week, so I suggest French bread—three loaves. She can freeze two.

On the fourth day True Love gifts four calling birds. According to my clever friend Google, calling birds are actually European blackbirds, but try singing that nine times. Considering the migratory habits of calling birds, I think calling cards might last longer. Plus it works in the song.

On day five True Love sends a real gift: five golden rings. Finally, a gift his girlfriend can enjoy—or hock after they break up.

He should really stop right there, but no. On the sixth day of Christmas True Love shows up with six geese a-laying. By now his lady is becoming concerned by her man's sudden interest in fowl, especially when he gives her seven swans a-swimming the very next day. At this point she might find a traditional gift reassuring. Maybe slippers and a robe. No fruit cake though. She's already got one of those.

If she hasn't moved out without leaving a forwarding address by day eight, our lucky recipient will receive eight maids a-milking. This would be a very useful gift if she has a dairy. If not, this is no time to give her cows. I suggest skipping the milk maids, instead presenting his darling with a nice assortment of cheeses.

On day nine he presents nine ladies dancing. Let me just say, anytime your true love shows up with dancing ladies, there's going to be trouble. The ten lords a-leaping scheduled to arrive the next day may help ease the tension by giving the ladies someone else to dance with. But True Love could save himself a lot of explaining if he'd just take his girlfriend dancing.

Having learned nothing during his gift giving spree, True Love sends an entire pipe and drum corps on days eleven and twelve. Before the neighbors complain, his beloved could announce to the musicians, "Put down your instruments everyone and come paint my house." That would be a lovely gift.

Tales from the Garage

Greetings, friends!

A lot of people talk about their travel adventures in their Christmas letters but I didn't do much traveling this year. In fact, my car barely left the garage so I'll tell you about what happened there instead.

One day this past summer a snake dropped onto the hood of my car as I was pulling into my garage. It was exactly like a scene from *Raiders of the Lost Ark* except it was a baby snake and I wasn't wearing a fedora and carrying a bull whip when I got out to look. Also I screamed, and I don't remember Indiana Jones doing that in the movie.

I couldn't tell if it was a rattlesnake or not and it wouldn't let me get close enough to check—not that I would have. I'm no snake expert, but I'm pretty sure it wasn't any happier about the situation than I was. As I was considering my options it slithered into the hole at the base of the windshield wiper.

I leaped out of the car and called a mechanic to ask if there was any way the snake could get inside my car from its hiding place. He assured me there was not, but for weeks I watched the floorboards as much as I watched the road ahead. I don't recommend that.

In other wildlife news, one morning I saw a wolf spider the size of a Chihuahua in the garage. I considered putting it on a leash and giving it to my son. He's always wanted a dog. But alas, the spider got away. Where a critter that large can hide, I can't imagine. I'm afraid I'll go out to the garage one morning and it will be backing my car out.

Our power went out one day in July just as I was about to leave for a meeting. Our garage door does have an emergency pull for such an occasion, but either it didn't work right or I didn't. I called to tell the people I was meeting with that I would be late because I was trapped in my garage. In retrospect I think I could have worded it differently. When I finally made it to the meeting I was bombarded with comments about my daring escape from the bowels of my garage. Apparently they've seen my garage.

Still on the garage theme, in May we had a recall notice for my car's brake light switch. Shortly after that work was done a dashboard warning light came on. According to the manual, the light meant something called "hill assist" was no longer working. I hadn't realized I had such a thing, so I certainly didn't know what it did—until it didn't do it anymore. Apparently "hill assist" helps keep my car from rolling back when I take off on a hill, a challenge when you drive a vehicle with a manual transmission as I do. All this time I thought I was just that good.

If that weren't bad enough, all the other warning lights came on shortly thereafter. My dash looked like a Christmas tree. Fortunately the lights went off when I turned the car off. Unfortunately, the taillights didn't. They stayed on all night and the battery died. My car had to be towed to the dealership to recover from its recall repair.

Speaking of transmissions, the one on our washing machine went kaput in July. Up until that point I'd been blissfully unaware that my washing machine had a transmission. Without it, my poor washer tried to spin and agitate at the same time. You try that sometime!

The result was that all my clothes tied themselves in knots while they were washing. Then I was agitated. We replaced the washer with a fancy front-loader that has a window and more settings than my smart phone has apps. The only way this washer could be any better is if it dried, folded and put the clothes away for me.

Incidentally, I have to compliment the delivery men. They got my new washing machine through my jungle of a garage and into the laundry room without hurting themselves, breaking anything or swearing even once. Even more impressive, they had the good manners not to look shocked when they pulled the old one out and saw how it looked underneath. In the hierarchy of housekeeping, cleaning under my appliances doesn't even make the list. And nothing is more embarrassing than having other people see what's under your appliances after twenty-plus years— except maybe flagging down a passing motorist while wearing Velcro rollers and a bathrobe.

My phone rang at six o'clock one morning a few weeks ago. It was still dark. My husband was just backing out of the garage and the call was for him. I opened the front door, jumped up and down, waved, hollered and generally made a fool of myself to get him to notice before he drove away. It worked. The truck stopped and pulled back into the driveway. That's when I realized it wasn't my husband's truck. Someone was using our driveway to turn around. I'll bet they don't do that again.

Anyway, along with my new washing machine I also practically got a new house and a new car this year too. Actually what I got was a new roof, some new siding and $8,000 worth of car repairs after a doozy of a hailstorm in August. People who know we have a two-car garage wonder why my car was damaged. I'll tell you why. Because it wasn't in the garage.

I was out and about when I heard the storm warning on the radio. I raced home, pulled up to my garage, hit the remote and watched as the door lifted to reveal that some-one else was parked in my spot. I won't mention any names but it was someone I'm married to. His half of the garage was taken up by a building project he'd been working on for months so there was no point in asking if he could wrap it up and move it out before the storm hit.

Now you can see why I didn't leave my garage much after that. I didn't want to lose my parking place again. Anyway, merry Christmas to you and yours. I hope things are well in your garage, your laundry room and your life.

With warm regards,

Indiana Jones

It's the Thought That Counts, So Make Sure You're Thinking

AAH, THE PERFECT GIFT. Your loved one will cherish it for years to come. They'll tell everyone they know about it. And they'll think of you fondly every time they use it, which you hope will make up for the way they think of you the rest of the time.

But time is running out. At this point you're far more likely to purchase one of the following types of gifts for your loved one. They'll tell everyone about these too.

1. The gift you give because you want the receiver to have it. In fact, you *need* the receiver to have it—like when you give your spouse cooking lessons or a messy co-worker a desk organizer or your college-aged child a broom for his dorm room. You're convinced that if you wrap a razor or a gift

certificate for tattoo removal in beautiful paper and put a giant bow on it, the recipient will see it as a thoughtful gift instead of what it really is: an underhanded way to bring them around to your way of thinking.

2.   The gift you give because you want it for yourself. Based on the shape, size and weight of the packages under your tree, you're pretty sure no one got it for you so you buy it on a whim. You feel guilty immediately, as you should. But you tell yourself the same story you plan to tell your spouse: You bought them the $400 fishing rod or the Make Your Own Greek Yogurt Kit so that the two of you can spend more quality time together. The danger is that, out of spite, they may not even let you have it in the divorce.

3.   The gift you give because you don't have a single idea and you're flat out of time to come up with one. The pressure is on. The store is crowded with panicked shoppers fighting over the last Stinky Pig game. You've heard the Chipmunks sing "Christmas Don't Be Late," one too many times over the intercom. And you know that if you don't get out of this store fast someone's going to get run over and not by a reindeer. You vow that next year you'll "know before you go." But this year you start tossing gadgets into your cart: a decorative toilet paper dispenser complete with AM/FM radio, clock and emergency siren; an alarm clock that will scold your teenager out of bed; a scale that politely informs whoever is standing on it that they've gained weight.

Stop! There's another way. At times like this, wise shoppers opt for gift cards. You may think gift cards are a cop-out but they have many advantages, the main one being that if you and your recipient aren't speaking by Christmas you can use the gift yourself. Not so if you bought left-handed golf clubs and you're right-handed. Or a small Minnesota Vikings sweatshirt and you're an extra-large.

Gift cards are easy to wrap and one size really does fit all. Plus they save you from buying one of those last minute, desperate attempts at a gift, like a set of fuzzy dice or a lawn elf.

And gift cards are practical. Those who don't have much can use them to buy things they need; those who have everything can use them to buy more things they don't need. Maybe they could even buy you something.

I admit gift cards do have some drawbacks though. For one thing they show the recipient how cheap you are. Of course they may already know that. Also gift cards aren't much fun to shake under the tree. I suggest you wrap them together with something else, say a box of candy or a large rock.

You can't buy gift cards on sale like you can actual gifts. They aren't cheaper by the dozen and you can't buy one, get one free. A twenty-dollar gift card is always going to cost you twenty dollars. I take that back. The last twenty-dollar gift card I bought cost around twenty-one dollars because of a handling fee. Unfortunately the recipient will still think I only spent twenty dollars on them...unless I tell them—which I might.

And gift cards are often a wash. You give your brother a ten-dollar gift card and he gives you a ten-dollar gift card.

Or worse, you give him a ten-dollar gift card and he gives you a twenty-dollar gift card. Or worse yet, you give him a twenty-dollar gift card and he gives you a five-dollar gift card. Ouch.

Finally, it might be a slippery slope letting people shop for their own gifts. I picture a day when everyone on my gift list just hands me a receipt and asks me to reimburse them.

Making Peace with Lefse

UFFDAH, NORWEGIANS take their lefse seriously! I married into a family of Scandinavian descent (half Norwegian, half Swedish), and it was at my first Christmas dinner with my in-laws more than thirty years ago that I learned just how seriously they take it. I foolishly mentioned that being of German descent, I had never actually tasted lefse. All conversation stopped. I think someone may have kicked my husband under the table. I know they all glared at him. To this day some of his family members still wonder why he married me. But it may not be the lefse.

For those of you who are unfamiliar with it, lefse is one of those traditional foods that often shows up during the holiday season. It's a type of flatbread made mostly with potatoes and flour. And it's not only a delicacy but a source of great pride to the Norwegians in my life. I've never taken my brats and sauerkraut that seriously because... well... how could I?

My father was full-blooded German and my mother was half German. Together they made homemade sauerkraut and a wonderful sausage that I would love to taste again. But sauerkraut and sausage were never served at our holiday dinners. So I do admire those who keep the traditional recipes alive—whether they're worth keeping alive or not.

I'm teasing! It's not that I don't like lefse. The truth is I'm neutral about it. I could take it or leave it, just like I could take or leave white bread, tortillas and wallpaper paste. They're just not worth getting worked up over.

In my uneducated opinion there are many other fine Scandinavian foods that are much more deserving of the devotion my in-laws have for their lefse. My mother-in-law has passed away, but she used to serve many of them for holiday meals. I loved her flat bread. Her Swedish meatballs were fabulous. And I was crazy about her klubb, or as I like to call them, potato bowling balls. Kidding! They're potato dumplings and they're amazing. You don't feel much like swimming or dancing for several hours after enjoying them but you're very happy anyway.

I can even find something to like about lutefisk: melted butter. For those fortunate enough to be unacquainted with it, lutefisk is prepared by soaking dried cod in lye to tenderize it, then boiling it to a gelatinous consistency. There are food words that go together naturally—"roast" and "beef," "scrambled" and "eggs." But "gelatinous" and "fish" aren't two of them.

One should be respectful of a family's traditional holiday foods but I don't care much for lutefisk. I don't think my in-laws do either but they still often feel a primal need to serve it at holiday meals.

It's the lefse that shows up at every Christmas meal though, and I just can't get excited about it. Yet I've seen wars fought over it. Family feuds anyway. Do you use butter alone or butter and sugar on your lefse? Do you cut it into small pieces or leave the circle intact for serving? Is it okay to spread margarine instead of butter on your lefse or is that a sacrilege?

I heard a story of a wayward daughter-in-law who was practically disowned because she made her lefse using instant mashed potatoes. And I heard of another young wife whose husband almost left her because she filed her lefse recipe in the recipe box under "Foreign Foods."

Interestingly, I also heard about a Norwegian exchange student who expressed surprise that anyone in the United States even makes lefse since none of her acquaintances back in Norway do anymore.

Early in my marriage my mother-in-law gave me a griddle for making lefse. And I have used it often—to make pancakes. As long as there's a Sons of Norway chapter in this town I see no reason to learn to make lefse.

But in the interest of family unity I've developed some recipes for making lefse more palatable to me the next time we host my in-laws for Christmas dinner:

Norwegian S'more: Wrap chocolate bars and marshmallows in lefse.

After School Snack Lefse: Spread peanut butter and jelly on lefse. Roll up and slice into bite-sized chunks for the children to play with.

And my personal favorite, German/Norwegian Alliance Lefse: Spread lefse with butter. DO NOT substitute margarine. Drain sauerkraut and spread over buttered lefse. Top sauerkraut with diced bratwurst. Sprinkle with course ground black pepper. Enjoy brats and sauerkraut. Discard lefse.

Santa, I've Forgiven You for the Barbie I Never Got

Dear Santa,

I know you haven't heard from me since I wrote to ask for that Barbie doll all those years ago. I might have written you more if I'd gotten it. But I'm finally willing to give you another chance.

Before I get into all I want for Christmas though, can I make a suggestion? I don't mean to be critical but seeing us when we're sleeping and knowing when we're awake is a little creepy. I wouldn't sleep the rest of the night if I ever caught you peeking through my window at 2 a.m. Just something to think about, sir.

Also, I know you're gonna find out who's naughty and nice, and I think I can help you with that. In the naughty camp, you can put litterers, spammers and identity thieves. Also shoppers who leave their grocery carts in the middle of the parking lot, people who spit out their gum on the sidewalk and anyone who doesn't return my phone calls.

On the nice side are volunteers, medical professionals, first responders and people who share their Christmas baking with me. Oh, and me. I'm nice—on most days. Or at least on some days. So when you're making your list and checking it twice, would you please consider the following?

I don't need much. In fact, I was thinking since your sleigh will be empty on the way home maybe you could haul a few things away for me. Then next year your elves could refurbish them for someone else who doesn't need them either.

I would like a new snow blower though. We had one but it worked best in light fluffy snow, which is exactly the same kind of snow I work best in. The heavy, wet stuff that fell last year did us both in, but one of us didn't get to quit.

I have a smart phone and I love it. So Santa, I'm wondering if I could have a smart smoke detector—one that can tell the difference between a kitchen fire and a little cheese spilled in the bottom of my oven. And how about a smart shredder that could warn me if I was about to shred my Social Security card? And maybe a smart spellchecker that knows what I mean to type, because even though they're both spelled correctly, being "inducted" into the Hall of Fame is very different from being "indicted" into the Hall of Fame.

Also could I have a year's supply of sunglasses and winter gloves? I know for some people that means a pair of each. But I'd need a lot more than that. I regularly leave sunglasses and gloves at locations all over town and I never notice until it's too late to remember where I've been. What I don't understand is why I need my sunglasses and gloves going in, but not coming back out.

And Santa, I need a new purse. But not just any purse; my new purse should look very small on the outside but be very large on the inside. Come to think of it, I'd like some shoes like that too.

I'm not sure you could arrange this, but I wish all vehicles could have two horns. I know we need the loud obnoxious one for emergencies, but I'd also like a kinder, gentler one that wouldn't scare the bejeebers out of an absent-minded driver who is simply lost in thought when the light turns green. I hate that.

You might not be able to do anything about this either, Santa, but is there any way bacon could be good for me? And Cheetos? And ice cream with hot fudge, caramel sauce and peanuts sprinkled on top?

Also I think there should be more almonds in Almond Joys. I love almonds but four doesn't seem all that joyful to me.

And I'd like ice cream bars with chocolate coating that doesn't fall off when I bite and also bread without crusts. I know a lot of people like the crusts, so in the spirit of the season I'll save mine for them. I told you I was nice.

How to Wrap a Million Dollar Smartphone

YOU CAN'T TELL BY LOOKING at my wrapping, but I was once a professional gift wrapper. Sort of. When I was a teenager, I worked at a hardware store in my hometown, Buffalo, South Dakota. Buffalo had a population of around 350 people and was many miles from a department store. Also I was in high school before the days of online shopping—about a hundred years before the days of online shopping. So the hardware store carried a variety of housewares, toys and other items that were often purchased for gift giving. We also had a fabulous selection of wrapping paper and bows but only a few people on staff who could really do them justice. I wasn't one of them.

Practice should make perfect and I wrapped many gifts, but they always had those big bulges on the sides of the package where the paper comes together—like I accidentally wrapped a hammer in there, which I may have once or twice. Even today I turn a gift on its side and put a big bow on the lump to cover it up.

But I can finally feel good about my wrapping, and not because it's gotten better. Recently I've read about several studies that suggest attractive gift wrapping can backfire by leading the receiver to anticipate an equally attractive gift. That means that when they open your beautifully wrapped package and find an egg slicer or a hair removal device, they're bound to be disappointed. They might be disappointed anyway.

But researchers say fancy wrapping can even dim the enthusiasm of someone receiving a nice gift. Meanwhile, mediocre wrapping can enhance the joy of receiving any gift because the wrapping hasn't built up expectations, though I don't think anything could enhance the joy of receiving a hair remover or an egg slicer.

It makes sense really. Imagine that a month before Christmas you receive a gift that's been professionally wrapped in gold metallic wrapping paper with a red satin ribbon and a giant bow. You see it under your tree every day and you can't help imagining all the wonderful things that could be in that package. Crystal? A new camera? A hundred-dollar bill and a big rock to add weight to the package? You can't wait for Christmas!

Finally, it's time. You tear into the package prepared to be wowed, and you find...a hot dog cooker or a snow cone maker. Naturally you're disappointed. Who wants snow cones in December?

If these studies had been done back when I was a professional gift wrapper it would have saved me a lot of embarrassment. I could have handed my customers their lumpy packages and said, "If your wife is disappointed that you bought mixing bowls for her birthday, don't blame me."

According to one researcher there's an exception to the gift wrap rule, and that's when the value of your gift isn't obvious. For example, let's say you're giving your teenager the $1.3 million Diamond Crypto Smartphone. If she thinks the diamonds are cubic zirconia she might carelessly misplace her phone under her bed or accidentally throw it in with the dirty laundry. In order to signal that the gift actually *does* have great value you should definitely have it professionally wrapped. You should also have your head examined.

For gifts valued at less than $1.3 million, consider more humble wrapping:

- Wrap your gift in newspaper, being careful to avoid the obituary page.
- Wrap it in brown paper and tie it up with string while humming a verse of "My Favorite Things."
- Make the wrapping part of the gift. For example, use a tea towel to wrap a package of kitchen sponges.
- Go wrapless—the gift, not you.
- My personal favorite though, is the gift bag. Gift bags are attractive but not so much that they raise my expectations. They don't require any special wrapping skill when I go to reuse them later. And they make it easy for me to peek.

All I Wanted for Christmas and Didn't Get

MY TIRES WENT FLAT, my oven died and my printer stopped printing—all just before Christmas. This was lucky because I was able to hint to everyone I know that all I wanted for Christmas was a new gas oven, a new printer and a new set of tires. Some people think practical items like these don't make good gifts but those people have never priced gas ovens.

I guess my hints weren't clear enough because I didn't find tires, a printer or an oven under my tree. It's not too late. I would still graciously accept all the above for early birthday gifts. My birthday isn't until August, but even I can't do without an oven that long.

Honestly I don't see how I could have worn our oven out. When it started taking longer to finish the job I thought it was because of the dust that's settled in it. Just to be sure I called a very nice oven repairman. He said it wasn't the dust. We both thought he'd fixed the problem but my Thanksgiving turkey didn't agree. Neither did the guests I'd invited to eat it.

So, I called the oven technician again. He did what he could, but in the end he pronounced my oven terminal. He told me it may work for a while but it won't be very reliable—much like the cook who uses it. That was three weeks before Christmas. Some people would see this as a problem, but where other people see a problem I see an opportunity—the opportunity to get out of baking. Now that the Christmas baking season is over I could really use a new oven. Hint, hint.

My printer has been making more noise than seems necessary lately. It's also been giving me error messages about something called an ink pump which sounds vital in a printer. Sometimes the printer prints, but more and more often it does not. The problem seemed to get worse just at that time when organized people were copying Christmas letters for those they care about. I care about people too, but my printer wasn't working. Also I didn't write a Christmas letter.

Around that time, my front driver's side tire was low. I limped to the tire shop where the tire man told me the problem was the bead. Did I know what a bead is? "Yes," I said. "I know beads when I see them but what does that have to do with my tire?"

"The bead," he said, "refers to the edge of the tire that sits on the wheel." Oh. Even I can see why it would be better if it sat there right.

He fixed the tire but a few days later my front passenger side tire was low. This time the problem was a nail. I do know what a nail is. The tire man fixed that too, but he told me nails and beads are the least of my worries. I said, "I know! Both my oven and my printer aren't working."

He said that I should add to the list that my tires need replacing. I refused to believe it. Everything can't fall apart at once, can it? Someone suggested I try the penny test to see for myself. You place a penny upside down in the tire tread and if you still see all of Lincoln's hair you need new tires. My good friend Google said a quarter works even better. I haven't purchased a new printer or a new gas oven yet, so I still have some pennies and quarters left. And after consulting with Lincoln and Washington, both wise presidents with fine heads of hair, I decided that yes, I do indeed need new tires.

I guess that's how life is sometimes. You're going along fine when suddenly your Thanksgiving turkey takes an extra hour to cook, your printer stops printing and politicians can no longer hide in your tire tread. Don't feel bad for me. But if you do, send pennies and quarters. A lot of them. Hint, hint.

Yule Be Sorry

SO YOU TURNED THE HUNT for a Christmas tree into a family field trip to the forest. Good for you! Then you lost the ax and fought all the way back to town over the merits of spruce versus pine.

And you were the only one in a twelve-block radius who didn't light up your house like Las Vegas. But that's only because you couldn't remember where you put the lights after you fell off the ladder last year.

Once again, you didn't get your Christmas letter mailed. Naturally you had a good reason for that: you didn't write one. Thankfully you still received plenty of Christmas cards and letters. That's because your friends and family are more efficient than you are. It would appear from their lengthy Christmas letters that they're also more interesting.

You were determined to see your children's Christmas program this year so you arrived at the auditorium a full hour early only to be told that all the seats in the first twenty rows were already taken. You took a seat in row twenty-one and still had fifty minutes to wait. Then you could only catch glimpses of your kids every now and then when the heads in front of you all lined up just right. As it turned out, they didn't sing anyway.

You heard that the average person gains a few pounds during the holiday season. You were determined not to be average and you weren't. You were above average—maybe because your holiday season started with the Halloween candy.

Last year you vowed you'd have all your Christmas shopping done by December 1. You even bought one gift on sale last January. Eleven months later you couldn't find it, nor could you remember what it was or who it was for.

That meant that once again you had none of your shopping done with just days to go before Christmas. And you weren't alone which was no comfort at all. There were at least four hundred people in the first store you visited. And it didn't make you feel like someone with the Christmas spirit when you nearly came to blows with one of them over the last air fryer on the shelf. What else could you do? It was the only gift you were sure of.

In desperation you bought five gift cards and six cheese trays for your remaining list. You spent an afternoon feeling like a failure, wrapping cheese trays and large boxes holding nothing but gift cards. You did feel clever about that—until you ran out of paper and had to unwrap some of the large boxes and move the gift cards to smaller boxes. Then you ran out of tape.

A friend came by bearing a gift. This cheered you momentarily until you remembered that you had nothing for her. You thought fast—gift card or cheese tray? Reluctantly you handed her a cheese tray—a cheese tray that was intended for someone else. As she unwrapped it you mumbled, "I know how much you like cheese." Meanwhile you were wondering if she was lactose intolerant—and when you'd have time to go back to the store for another cheese tray and more tape.

You got your feelings hurt when you won your company's Ugly Christmas Sweater Contest without even entering. You decided to wear a tank top to work on the day of the contest next year to avoid any confusion.

The Christmas bonus you expected turned out to be a fruit basket and one of the oranges was rotten. You caught the flu and missed your Christmas party. And you lost your temper and called Santa Claus a big fat fake in front of your five-year-old. Frankly you'll be relieved when the holiday season is over.

But don't be so hard on yourself. Focus on the reason for the season. And take comfort in the fact that you aren't alone. (I'm right there with you.) Finally, remember there's still time to make some fabulous New Year's resolutions.

No Way to Start
a New Year

HAPPY NEW YEAR TO YOU AND YOURS! I hope you rang it in at a raucous gathering with lots of friends and loud music. Unless you're like me. Then I hope you didn't. Then I hope you had a quiet evening with a few loved ones and fell asleep early despite the racket next door.

I'm a morning person, which means New Year's Day is more meaningful to me than New Year's Eve if only because I'm awake for it. If I sleep past six on New Year's Day, I feel like the year is off to a bad start. And if I saw the new year in at all, it was only because I woke up at midnight to use the bathroom.

My personal tradition is to bid the old year a gentle goodnight around ten o'clock, then wake up before my family does on New Year's Day and sit by the Christmas tree with my cat, my caffeine and my journal. I write about what I accomplished during the past year—which doesn't take long—and where I fell short—which does.

The fun part is writing about what I'm looking forward to in the new year. At that point I still have the optimism that accompanies New Year's Day—a glorious feeling that I'll have until at least January 2.

I suspect my quiet morning New Year's ritual puts me in the minority. A quick internet search reveals hundreds of New Year's Eve traditions here and around the globe and many fewer for New Year's Day, probably because so many people are sleeping off their hangovers.

There are some common ingredients of New Year's celebrations here and abroad: alcohol, food, fireworks, alcohol, kissing, bells, resolutions and alcohol. As the designated driver at every party I attend, I can only guess that alcohol allows the revelers to forget the worst of the past year and start the new one off just as badly.

My family doesn't have any particular New Year's food traditions, though we do always eat something. But food traditions around the world run the gamut from grapes to seafood to sauerkraut. In some countries they hide coins or other objects in their food and it's believed that if you find one, you'll have good luck in the new year—unless you choke or break a tooth which is no way to start a new year.

One of the most prominent celebrations in our country is the ball drop held in New York City's Times Square. I've dropped the ball many times but I've never considered it anything to celebrate. Still the popularity of this spectacle has inspired many other drop events. There's the Peach Drop in Georgia, the Music Note Drop in Nashville and the Possum Drop in Brasstown, North Carolina. You'll be relieved to learn that the celebratory possum is lowered over the noisy crowd in a transparent box rather than dropped. That would be a terrible way to begin a new year if you're a possum.

In parts of South Africa they don't drop balls, peaches or possums; they throw the furniture. Throwing old furniture out the window symbolizes casting out the old and starting fresh. Italians throw old kitchen crockery and other items out the window for the same reason. Neither tradition is as common as it once was though, maybe because it wasn't the best way to start a new year for anyone walking by the window. Furniture and crockery stores appreciated it though.

In parts of the world—Malaysia, the Balkans, the Middle East, parts of Afghanistan and elsewhere—some folks ring in a new year with celebratory gunfire. One hopes those shooting haven't had too much champagne.

There are many other unusual traditions for wrapping up an old year and kicking off a new one—wearing yellow underwear in Venezuela and red ones in Italy and Spain, breaking plates in Denmark, and walking around with an empty suitcase in Ecuador. Yes, it's peculiar but it beats lugging around a full one.

Finally, there's that ubiquitous tradition of making New Year's resolutions. There is something about starting a new year that inspires us all. Suddenly all things are possible. We are motivated, enthusiastic and confident. Overnight we feel like we've gained the power to change ourselves and transform our lives. This is the year we finally become the people we've always wanted to be.

Then comes January 2. Talk about dropping the ball. You can almost hear the collective sigh as people everywhere fail at whatever it is they resolved to do. It's the "oops" heard around the world.

And it's a terrible way to start a new year. Vowing to get fit, get organized, save money and spend more time with our family is a lot of pressure to put on ourselves—and our family—especially when we're still recovering from New Year's Eve. But if we can't let the resolution tradition die, I suggest we start making them in late December so we won't have to live with them so long.

I Like You Very Much
but Please Go

FOR THOSE OF US WHO'VE BEEN CRAVING a little silent night since Thanksgiving there was World Introvert Day on January 2. And I missed it. Introverts being introverts I guess no one was out there promoting it.

World Introvert Day has been around for more than a decade and I've just learned about it myself. Apparently it was the brainchild of psychologist and author Felicitas Heyne who decided rightly that introverts needed a day to go dormant after the holiday season. Had I known about it sooner I would have holed up at home on January 2. Oh wait. That's what I did.

I'm an introvert myself, which comes as a surprise to some people who know me. That's because they don't understand introverts. Extroverts sometimes confuse introversion with shyness. They think all introverts blush when we talk to other people and hide in the bathroom during our own birthday parties. I've never done that. That's no place to eat birthday cake.

Some extroverts think introverts are unfriendly, even rude. They think we keep our blinds closed all day and grouse at the neighborhood children to stay off our lawns. I'll have you know the three young boys who live next door to me regularly play on my lawn. And I'm hardly ever rude, except in traffic.

Introversion is simply a difference in our brains which I won't go into because I'm an introvert not a scientist. But I can tell you this: Introverts are renewed from within through solitude and reflection while extroverts recharge by being around people and other outside stimuli, much of which introverts find appalling—the stimuli, not the people. We like people, just not when they run in packs or come to our door unexpectedly.

An introvert would rather email than call someone and when we do call we're not disappointed when we have to leave a message.

We like to shop in stores where there aren't very many other customers. Unfortunately our favorite stores don't stay in business long.

We'd rather go to lunch with one or two friends than go to a dinner party or, heaven forbid, a mixer. Introverts are afraid mixers are how we'll spend all eternity if we die and go to hell.

I worked in several restaurants when I was young and as an introvert I preferred my job as a dishwasher to the one I had waiting tables. Unfortunately no one tips the dishwasher.

I don't tell my extroverted friends when my husband is going out of town because they'll think I want company. I love my husband but I treasure my time alone. He doesn't take it personally because he feels the same way. I hope it's because he's an introvert too.

Some experts estimate that up to 50 percent of the population are introverted though no one knows for sure because introverts tend to avoid surveyors.

According to my research some really successful people are introverts, including Meryl Streep, Steve Martin and J.K. Rowling. Rosa Parks, Mahatma Gandhi, Albert Einstein, Eleanor Roosevelt and Abraham Lincoln were all supposedly introverts too. None of them could have accomplished all they did if they'd been out partying every night.

Most billionaires including Warren Buffett, Elon Musk, Bill Gates and Dorothy Rosby are introverts too. I was just seeing if you were paying attention.

You extroverts who've read this far may be wondering why there isn't a special holiday for you. Listen to yourself. Every holiday is for you. Name one major holiday where the tradition is to stay home and read a good book.

I'd go so far as to say we live in an extrovert's world. Why do you think there are stadiums, bus tours, shopping malls and open office spaces? If I worked in one of those I'd get even less work done than I do now.

You may also be wondering how the introverts in your life will observe World Introvert Day next year and will there be a party. No there will not. That doesn't mean we won't be celebrating the day though. We'll just be doing it quietly and separately.

Blue Christmas

Belated Holiday Greetings!

Yes, I realize I'm very late getting my Christmas letter out, but there's a good reason for that: I'm late writing it.

We have much to be grateful for in the Rosby household. None of us had any major injuries, serious illnesses or cavities last year. Our only health problems were minor ones, although a cold did cause me to miss two Christmas parties. This was disappointing because I heard later that the food was excellent at both and that there was mistletoe at one of them. But I felt I should stay home and keep my germs to myself and anyway, I'd lost my voice. Who wants to stand around and let everyone else do the talking all night?

Yes, I ended the year with a case of laryngitis and a houseful of guests. I'm not sure but it seems like they enjoyed their stay more because of it. I found myself weighing the importance of every word I wanted to speak against the pain, and most times I decided it wasn't worth the effort. I resolved to continue considering my words as carefully after my voice returned and so far I've kept that resolution as well as I kept all the others.

Incidentally my cold also put the kibosh on my Christmas shopping. On the bright side, this saved me a lot of money which I was able to use on a terrific new set of casserole dishes. And it was about time. Every single casserole dish my husband and I received when we were married has been broken. Fortunately the manufacturer says our new set is virtually unbreakable and that appears to be true—for all but one lid. So far.

In March we painted and put new carpet in our office and bedrooms. And by "we" I mean my husband who painted and the carpet guy who laid the carpet. My job was to help pick colors. I voted for blue everything and my husband agreed. He'd read that blue is calming and I guess he thought I needed that.

The timing was good because shortly after I moved back into my office, our internet went down. I needed to call my provider to get help but I didn't know their number and I couldn't search for it online because, well, my internet was down. I tracked down an old phone book and discovered that the number wasn't in it. If I hadn't been standing in my new soothing blue office, I might have been really upset. Oh wait.

I'd barely regained my composure when one of us—I'm not saying who—spilled an entire eight-ounce glass of cranberry juice on the old carpet in our basement just days after it had been cleaned. Unfortunately, it's cream colored and not soothing at all. Thanks to quick thinking and an entire bottle of stain remover, now you can hardly tell it happened. But when the lighting is just right you can barely make out what looks like a faint map of Australia on our carpet.

I received a speeding ticket this fall, which is always painful. This one was made even more embarrassing by the fact that my cell phone rang just as the officer came up to my car. Thankfully she didn't fine me as much as she could have. It may have worked in my favor that I kept the call short.

And I broke my glasses, which many people would consider clumsy. But anyone would have done the same thing under the circumstances; they were lying on the floor right where I stepped. After that I went into my new blue bedroom and sat for a really long time.

But all in all, things are not too bad. Another year has passed without my giving in to my husband's pleas for a Harley Davidson. Most of our friends and relatives are still speaking to us. And I have now gotten my Christmas letter done well before Valentine's Day.

Sincerely,

Dorothy, writing from my new blue office

The First Year of the Rest of Your Life

A FRIEND TOLD ME that her New Year's resolution is to live every day of next year as though it's her last day. I smiled and nodded. But inside I was thinking, "That's the dumbest New Year's resolution I've ever heard."

If she really lives every day like it's her last, she won't have any reason at all to have her oil changed or her teeth cleaned. Why stock up on groceries or clean the house? Let the mourners handle that. Certainly she wouldn't show up at work if it were the last day of her life. And who, on the last day of her life, would balance her checkbook or pay her parking tickets, both of which I'm resolving to handle better this year. If my friend carries through on her resolution, she'll wake up next January 1 with no job, bad teeth and a boot on her front tire.

Despite the obvious drawbacks I've heard a lot of people espouse the "live like it's your last day" philosophy—at least in theory. Not me. Self-fulfilling prophesies being what they are, I'd worry that with too much living like it's my last day it might happen a lot sooner than I'd like.

But there is one thing I appreciate about my friend's resolution: it renders all others unnecessary. I heard that three of the most common resolutions are to lose weight, exercise and quit smoking. I can't speak for smokers, but I know I wouldn't spend my last day counting carbohydrates or riding an exercise bike. Likewise, I wouldn't worry about giving up the caffeine or gnawing on my fingernails, other resolutions I've heard mentioned among my acquaintances.

Resolve to live like it's your last day and you'll never make another resolution again as long as you live, which may not be long.

I think what my friend and others like her are really saying is that they resolve to get their priorities in order during the New Year, especially those having to do with their relationships. That is a noble goal. But why don't they just say so? "You are more important to me than my job, my money or my bowling league," is a lot more endearing than "I'm living like I have only this day left and I think I can get along with you that long."

I suppose they also want to savor and enjoy each moment of whatever time they have left. This is understandable. But I prefer the "today is the first day of the rest of your life" philosophy. If you live like it's your first day rather than your last you'll probably have a little more enthusiasm about the prospect. You'll still have to pay your parking tickets and get some exercise but you'll get to keep your teeth.

The downside is that you may still feel compelled to make real New Year's resolutions. I'm here to help. In my quest to become a better person and avoid getting to my last day any sooner than I have to, I've thoroughly studied the topic of New Year's resolutions. And from my extensive research, I have gleaned the following tips for keeping them:

1. Write them down. The simple act of putting your resolutions on paper will make them seem more doable and make you feel more committed to them. Also, if you fail you'll have your list ready when it comes time to make resolutions next year.

2. Avoid taking on too much. Don't try to change everything about yourself all at once, even if your spouse wants you to.

3. Frame your resolutions in a positive way. For example, instead of saying "next year I will stop being a couch potato," say "I will become a couch asparagus, which has fewer carbohydrates."

4. Get a partner. If you've decided to get fit, enlist a friend with the same goal. That way you'll have someone to praise you when you're doing well, encourage you when you're not doing so well and go out for ice cream with you when you both give up.

5. Don't let setbacks discourage you. If you fall off the wagon get right back in the saddle! Tomorrow's another day. Never say die. Then next year resolve to stop using clichés.

6. Keep a journal of your progress. It could look something like this. January 1: I resolve to walk the dog daily. This is going to be so fun! January 2: Spotty and I walked four blocks. We are bonding and

getting fit at the same time! Tomorrow we'll do five. January 3: Spotty and I walked four blocks again. It's okay once we're walking but I hate getting up early. January 4: Spotty and I walked just two blocks today. It's so cold this time of year. January 5: I forgot to walk Spotty. January 6: Spotty isn't *my* dog. We got him for the kids. Let them walk him.

7.   Celebrate your successes! Finally got that credit card paid off? Congratulations! Now go buy new furniture. I'm kidding! But do celebrate. It's the first day of the rest of your life after all.

And the Winners Are...

IT WAS THE BEST OF LISTS. It was the worst of lists. Also the most, least, biggest, smallest, flattest and roundest of lists.

'Tis the season when experts on everything roll out their report cards of the past year. There are the usual suspects: Best Books, Worst Books, Best Movies, Worst Movies, Most Popular Baby Names, Most Popular Pet Names. And there are the unusual ones, for example the 20 Most Popular Dog Names That Would Totally Work for Your Kid Too. I didn't make that up.

Nor did I make up the Most Notable Cryptozoology Deaths, the Scariest Clowns or the Best Mannequin Pranks of the past year. Honest. And what a year it was for mannequin pranks.

There are the lists of best and worst products of the past year. For example, the Top 10 Cordless Pet Hair Vacuums, the Worst Technology and the 5 Best Snow Shovels of the past year. We use our regular vacuum to suck up cat hair so I had no idea there were enough pet hair vacuums to make a list. And I know without looking at the list what the best snow shovel is. It's the one anyone besides me is willing to use in my driveway.

There are the lists we all wish we could be on: The World's Highest Paid Athletes/Celebrities/Models and the People Who Mattered in the past year. It's worth noting they're not the same people.

There are lists of the 500 Richest People in the World and the Top 10 Smartest People in the World. I'm always happy to see there are more rich people than smart people on the list. It gives me hope for my financial future.

There's a list of the World's Most Beautiful People, which sounds like a good one to be on until you realize hardly anyone gets to be on it two years in a row. Either beauty truly is fleeting or being one of the world's most beautiful people really takes a lot out of you.

There are the lists you're relieved you're not on: Famous People Who Died, Biggest Celebrity Scandals (with photos) and Biggest Celebrity Breakups. That last one is full of surprises for me every year because I rarely know that the celebrities on the list have broken up. Sometimes I don't even know they were ever together. Or who they are.

There's the list of the Ten Most Embarrassing Moments of the past year (with video), which I'm proud to say I haven't been on — yet. I hope they never expand the list to twenty.

There's the list of the Dumbest Criminals of the Year. The top honor often goes to someone who was caught after posting photos from the crime scene on Instagram. Maybe "top honor" is a poor choice of words.

While I find these compilations fascinating I do have some issues with them. For one thing, their authors take great pleasure in listing the mistakes of others. There are the Worst Political Mistakes, Biggest Movie Mistakes, Biggest Password Mistakes and the Worst Celebrity Fashion Faux Pas of the past year. But there is no list of the biggest mistakes of list creators. Maybe I'll put that one together myself next year.

Also I think before someone somewhere creates the list of the Top 100 People of the Year or the Most Annoying TV Commercials there ought to be a vote. I wouldn't be much help with the Best Performing Stocks of the past year or the Top Ten Architectural Websites but I have some suggestions for the Dumbest People of the Year. Also the Dumbest Lists of the Year.

And why do we start seeing these efforts to sum up the past year in early November? I sympathize with list makers wanting to take the holidays off but how can they compile an accurate list representing an entire year before the year is over? A lot can happen on New Year's Eve.

No, list creators should definitely wait until January if they want to be fair and honest and include any embarrassing moments I have in late December.

I Learn the Hard Way
So You Don't Have To

I'M PROUD TO SAY I've developed a technique for putting in eye drops during the night without turning on the lights. Lucky for me, it doesn't work very well.

One night recently I woke up around 2 a.m. and reached for my drops. They weren't on the nightstand where I always put them—or where I always *intend* to put them. So I dug around in the dark until I found them in the drawer—or thought I did.

I took the lid off and using my not quite foolproof technique I aimed and squirted. Some went into my left eye and some missed and ran down my face—fortunately. Then I shot some into my right eye faster than you can say, "Dang! Why did that hurt so much?"

A lovely smell filled the air, but I didn't appreciate it fully because I was thinking that I normally don't smell anything when I put in eye drops. Also because my eyes were on fire.

By now you probably know where this is going. I was recently given a small bottle of lavender oil which the accompanying pamphlet claims is soothing and promotes sleep. And while that may be true, it is definitely not soothing in your eyes, nor does it promote sleep once you've put it in them.

I leapt out of bed, sprinted to the bathroom and stuck my face under the faucet. After splashing around in the sink for twenty minutes I sought comfort and additional first aid tips from that source of all knowledge, the internet. I don't believe the answer to every health question I find there but I'm always reassured to know I'm not the only person who's ever asked it.

It turns out plenty of people have gotten lavender oil in their eyes, though none in quite the direct manner I did it. Several sites recommended rinsing with milk so I tried that next and I did feel somewhat better. By then it was 3 a.m., my pajamas were soaked and I was out of milk. All the lavender oil in the world couldn't have soothed me back to sleep at that point.

I learned so much from this experience—mainly not to keep anything that could be mistaken for eye drops in my nightstand. It's a good thing I don't keep paint thinner by my bed.

I tell you this story because as we begin a new year I think it's important to reflect not only on the highlights of the past one but also on the dim lights. That way we won't be—how can I say this nicely—as dumb in the new year as we were in the old one.

As a public service I'd like to share some of the other lessons I learned last year. I hope this will save you from making the same mistakes I made, though I can't see most people making them.

For one thing, I learned that laundering money is fine if you do it in the washing machine. But I now know there are a lot of other things you should never run through the washer and dryer and the worst of all might be lip balm.

I now know that when you sweep off your steps you should never start on the bottom one. And that you should never get carried away using a paper shredder. And that you should always put the carrier back before you drive away from a drive-through bank.

I learned that if you're going to sit alone in your car in a busy parking lot and laugh like a maniac at something on the radio, you should hold your cell phone to your ear and pretend you're actually laughing with someone on the phone. That way things may go better for you once you get out of your car and go inside.

In the area of fashion and beauty I learned that when you check your look in the mirror you should remember you have a backside too. I was standing in line at the gas station one morning, and I had that strange sense that the other customers were looking at me. Turns out that's because they were. As I was getting back into my car I leaned back against the headrest and discovered I'd left a giant red Velcro roller in my hair. I cursed, tossed it into the back seat and headed to my meeting. A friend took one look at me and said, "Come here!" I did as I was told and she spun me around. "I know," I said. "My hair is a mess." I started to tell her what happened but she interrupted me to say, "No. Your skirt is unzipped." Oh.

I learned a few lessons in the kitchen this past year

and not just that I prefer eating out. I learned that if it can cut meat it can cut you, and that you can always add more chopped onion but it's really hard to pick out once you've added too much. Also you should check food often while you're cooking it because it's easier to go from rare to medium than it is to go from well-done to medium.

I understand now that loyalty doesn't pay. Or anyway it doesn't pay if you can't find your loyalty card when you need it. I have loyalty and membership cards for every hotel, convenience store and fast-food restaurant in the five-state region. I have the potential to save tens of dollars on buy-ten-get-one-free punch cards. And now I know I should locate them before I get to the counter. Other customers get antsy when you spend too much time looking through your card collection.

I made at least one other person mad last year. And unlike those in line behind me, this one was mad enough to say so. You know how when you're introduced to someone named Rudolf you're tempted to say, "You do have a very shiny nose"? Or when you meet someone named McDonald you're overcome with the urge to say, "E-I-E-I-O" or "Would you like fries with that?"

You're not? Well, I am and I know I'm not alone. I've heard "We're not in Kansas anymore" and "I'm going to get you and your little dog too!" so many times I nearly broke into a chorus of "Somewhere Over the Rainbow" just now thinking about it. I've never minded. That other Dorothy seems to help people remember my name and it beats going through life as What's Her Name.

I now understand that not everyone feels that way, thanks to someone else who has a movie name telling me so in a not-so-pleasant way. I won't say the name because he asked me never to use it again.

I learned many lessons in the area of technology this past year. For example, I learned that when your password doesn't work and then it doesn't work again and again, hitting the keys on your computer harder each time won't help. Instead you should pause, take a breath and calmly consider the possibility that you're using the wrong password.

I was reminded again that when you're working on your computer you should save early and save often. A document saved is a document you won't have to type all over again.

I learned that I should set my ancient dilapidated laptop on top of a stack of books so that other people at my online meeting will look me in the eyes rather than up my nose. And I learned that I should set it there *before* the meeting starts in case the battery falls out while I'm moving it.

I realize now that I should be more cautious when texting. For one thing, before you hit send you should make sure you're sending your text to the right person. Your boss might wonder what business you have telling her to pick up milk on the way home.

I also learned never to trust voice command or auto-correct. Incidentally I also learned that the year before last, and chances are good I'll learn it again next year. People get the wrong idea when you say, "I've been fine," but your voice-activated text gizmo types out, "I've been framed." Or you intend to say, "I love you," but your text reads, "I loathe you."

Don't worry; I didn't make that mistake but I can't print the one I did make. Let's just say I may have made another person mad last year.

A Better Way to Make New Year's Resolutions

I'M TRYING A NEW APPROACH to New Year's resolutions this year. Instead of worrying about everything I'd like to change about myself, I'm going to focus on what I'd like to change about everyone else. In other words, this year I'm making New Year's resolutions for other people. I don't know why I didn't think of it before. It's a lot more fun than the old way and I'm sure it will be every bit as effective.

For starters, I hereby resolve that hackers and identity thieves will use their considerable talents to contribute to society by pursuing legal employment. And if they don't, I resolve that law enforcement officials will track them down and put them behind bars where they'll be forced to listen to robo calls all day, every day for the rest of their sorry lives.

I resolve that spammers will stop spamming, scammers will stop scamming and litterers will stop littering. And I resolve that those who spit their gum on the sidewalk will be the ones who step on it later.

I resolve that TV viewers will begin questioning everything that comes out of the mouths of over-paid political pundits, and if they have any questions about who and what they should really believe, they'll call me and I'll tell them.

Likewise, I resolve that social media users will stop believing everything they read on Facebook and Twitter and that they'll refrain from sharing political rants and mean-spirited memes—unless I agree with them

And speaking of politics, I resolve that all eligible voters will vote in the next election. Or at least all eligible voters who see things my way will vote in the next election.

I hereby resolve that shoppers will no longer pick up items in one aisle, change their minds and leave said items in another aisle. I sympathize. I change my mind occasionally too. In fact the last time I went shopping I picked up a bag of sour cream and onion potato chips in aisle five and was overcome with guilt by the time I reached the produce department. But I got over it.

I resolve that as of January 1, other customers will cease unloading more items than are allowed in the express line and that they'll refrain from pointing it out if I do it.

And I resolve that shoppers will return their carts to the proper spot after they finish unloading their groceries instead of leaving them in the middle of the parking lot where I can back into them.

I resolve that other drivers will stop parking so close to the line in the parking lot that they can't help dinging my door when they get out of their car. And I resolve they'll find another parking place if it's me who parked too close to the line.

And finally I resolve that no one will ever again text and drive, drink and drive or get in my way when I drive. And that nobody will call me or come knocking at my door while I'm eating or sleeping, which I realize is a wide target. And that anyone who speaks on their cellphone within earshot of me will have the courtesy to make it an interesting conversation.

So there you have it: My new approach to making New Year's Resolutions. I think it will catch on. Soon everyone will be making resolutions for other people, and not just for strangers, but also for close friends and family. There are so many possibilities.

"I resolve that you'll stop interrupting."

"Yeah? Well, I resolve that you'll stop talking when I'm trying to interrupt."

"I resolve that you'll quit telling me how to drive."

"And I resolve that you'll learn to drive better."

"I resolve that you'll go back to making New Year's resolutions the old way."

"Well, I resolve that you'll learn to appreciate constructive criticism."

Resolve to Start Eating Better Next August

I HAD AN EPIPHANY this past Halloween. I was sitting alone, eating miniature candy bars from a giant bag of about 300. I got my usual number of trick-or-treaters: ten. Next year I should leave the lights on.

That wasn't the epiphany though. I already knew that. What I realized was that the overeating season doesn't start with the Thanksgiving turkey and end with the New Year's resolutions as I always thought. Here in the land of the free and the home of the plump, it actually runs from August to August with a couple of days of healthful eating in early January.

That's because the grocery stores put out their Halloween candy in August. We walk by, think, "It's too early for that," and then throw some in our cart. We're going to need to buy it eventually anyway. We're also going to need to buy it *again* eventually.

And that's how it starts. Friendly people set out dishes filled with candy corn and so-called "fun size" candy bars, which, if you ask me, would be way more fun if they were full size. Unfriendly people fill their candy dishes with gummy skulls and candy that looks like miniature bloody bones. Those wouldn't be much fun if they were full size.

Whatever they put in them, I admire people who have candy dishes—full candy dishes. Anyone can have an empty one. If I were going to have a full candy dish it would have to be filled with something I don't like. Maybe sardines.

You can find chocolate turkeys if you look hard but Thanksgiving isn't really about candy. Man—and woman—cannot live on candy alone. We need stuffing too. And pie.

Magically, right after Halloween the orange and brown candy wrappers are replaced by red and green foil—maybe by elves. And chocolate Santas and candy canes appear. By the way, if you ever give me Christmas candy, which would be a nice gesture, don't give me candy canes. I haven't liked those since a Christmas many years ago when I received a candy cane so big I'd probably still be eating it if it hadn't picked up lint so badly.

By Christmas the store-bought goodies are supplemented by homemade treats—except at my house. If we're going to have homemade treats someone else is going to have to make them and thankfully, someone often does. I'm lucky to have several friends who annually complain about holiday weight gain and doing their holiday baking in the same conversation.

We probably still have Christmas leftovers in our fridge on New Year's Day but we all make another big meal anyway. Then we diet—until January 3.

It helps that there's slim pickings for New Year's candy, though that's the only thing that's slim during the holiday season. You can get gummy shot glasses, chocolate champagne bottles and liquor-filled chocolates, but those aren't suitable for candy dishes—or children.

It's okay though. The pink and red candies, chocolate hearts and heart-shaped boxes are in stores by New Year's Day. Nothing says "I love you" like a giant box of chocolates, at least to me.

Early in our marriage my husband gave me chocolates every Valentine's Day. Then one year he gave me a box of candy he claimed he thought was chocolate. It turned out to be SweeTARTS. I'm sure I don't have to tell you how hard that was on our relationship.

It was after a little incident with chocolate mints that he switched to fresh flowers. Knowing how much I love them, he gave me a big box of Andes mints one Valentine's Day. On February 15 he asked if he could have some. No, he could not, and not because I wasn't willing to share—though I wasn't willing to share. They were gone. Roses are more expensive but they last longer and he gets to enjoy them too.

With the exception of a few green candies and some chocolate coins wrapped in gold foil, St. Patrick's Day isn't known for candy. But you can get corned beef and cabbage which is always a treat. Just don't put it in your candy dish.

The lack of St. Patrick's Day candy may be explained by the overabundance of Easter candy. Shortly after Valentine's Day, candy corns go pastel and chocolate bunnies appear. If you plan to give me Easter candy you should know I prefer solid chocolate bunnies to hollow ones. Apparently, to make a chocolate figure with no innards, you have to make it with brown crayons and I don't think we should eat those.

Hardly anybody gives away May baskets anymore, but if I ever do it I'll fill them with leftover candy canes and hollow Easter bunnies.

There are a few sweets that come wrapped in red, white and blue for Independence Day. And there are some peculiar candies that explode in your mouth, but those aren't treats as much as entertainment. This is the season for ice cream anyway—and going to the dentist.

I'm not aware of any Labor Day candy but no one misses it because the Halloween candy has been up since August.

Spread throughout the year are birthday parties, special events and the arrival of Girl Scout cookies which, in my opinion, should be a national holiday.

And so it goes. Every special occasion is followed by guilt, then resolve. We admit to ourselves we've really over-done it and promise to start fresh on New Year's Day. Or rather August 1.

The Super What?

I GREW UP THINKING MEN INVENTED football just to get out of doing dishes. I have seven brothers. Naturally there were a lot of dishes. And there was a mass exodus from the dining room to the living room on Sunday afternoons, so you can see how I might think that.

You can also see how, despite growing up with all those brothers, I didn't grow up to be a sports fan myself. It's simple. During games there was no room for me on the couch. And being number nine of ten, I was in no position to push anyone else off.

I'm not complaining though. When you have that many siblings you consider a majority of them corralled in one room for extended periods of time a welcome respite. A game on television meant my tormentors were accounted for, tethered to the TV, oblivious to my comings and goings. I could take long Sunday afternoon naps to the sound of a football game. I could use the only bathroom in our childhood home undisturbed. I could have friends over and trust they wouldn't be harassed. All was right in my little world—unless I walked in front of the television.

And my brothers were occupied for a long time on Sunday afternoons. I learned early that seven minutes left in a game could mean seventeen or twenty-seven. It never meant seven. Giving the time remaining in a football game is like giving your age in dog years.

That's why, while I may not be fond of professional sports in general and football in particular, I do like the sound of the broadcast. Far from exciting, however, I find it soothing and relaxing. It takes me back to a simpler time.

Mind you, it's the sound of the broadcast I like, not the sound of men yelling at players and officials who can't possibly hear them and wouldn't listen if they could. Over the years the sound of shouting has awakened me from many a sports-induced coma.

For ten years I worked as a radio announcer. I sat through a million sports broadcasts, or so it seemed, plugging in sponsor messages at the right moment (at least some of the time) and caring not a bit for the outcome of any game. But I loved the sound of the broadcast—just the sound. The finest compliment I could pay any of my sportscaster friends was, "You did such a good job I dozed off."

And occasionally I really did. More than once I awoke to a strange crackling sound—dead air, as it's known in the business.

The result of all of this is that I'm clueless about sports, though I am pretty good at dishes—when I set my mind to it. Baseball is my favorite of all professional sports, with its long periods of peace interrupted by occasional bursts of hysteria, much like life.

I like watching hockey but I don't care for the fights. I don't see why skating thirty-five miles an hour and maneuvering a puck the size of a quarter pounder through all those sticks and legs isn't enough for other fans.

I like tennis but I don't understand why zero is called "love." On those rare occasions when I play tennis I often have zero, but love is not what I'm feeling.

I like basketball. I even played it in high school for four years, though I'm no expert at it. I sat on the bench so much that, were it not for the pregame warmups, I wouldn't even have needed to shower.

But football remains the most mysterious of all sports to me. I have so many questions, the main one being why football fans say, "We won" or "We lost," when all they did was punch the couch cushions and curse the officials a few times.

This is all a very long way to explain why, when an acquaintance asked me who I'll be rooting for in the Super Bowl, I answered with a great deal of enthusiasm, "The what?" I was kidding. I know what the Super Bowl is. I just never know who's playing in it. Nor do I care. I do, however, know who is not playing in it.

I'm married to a man who, having grown up in Minnesota, loves the Minnesota Vikings more than he loves me or the Minnesota Twins. I think he might have mentioned it if the Vikings had made it to the Super Bowl this year.

Still, I'm sure that come Super Bowl Sunday he will join the hundred million or so people expected to watch the big game. I almost certainly will not, even though I have a dish-washer now and there's plenty of room on the couch for me.

I may join him for a few minutes though. There are a few things I like about Super Bowl Sunday, mainly the snacks. Some years I show up for the halftime show and some of the commercials are fun. But what I like best about the Super Bowl nowadays is the same thing I liked about football when I was growing up: me time. While the big game is on, I can come and go as I please—as long as I don't walk in front of the television.

Stand Up, Sit Down, Bite, Bite, Bite

BEFORE YOU CALL ME UN-AMERICAN for my lack of interest in the Super Bowl, you should know there's one thing I have in common with Super Bowl fans: guacamole. I love guacamole and apparently so do Super Bowl watchers. I read that 13.2 million pounds of avocados will be devoured on Super Bowl Sunday, making the event worthwhile even to me.

Apparently if you were to cover a football field with all the guacamole that will be consumed on Super Bowl Sunday, it would be an impressive 11.8 feet deep. I don't know why you would do that though; it would spoil the game and, more importantly, the guacamole.

The point is, it's a lot of guac and it's not all that Super Bowl fans will be eating. According to the keeper of all knowledge, the internet, Super Bowl Sunday is the second largest day for food consumption in the United States, with

Thanksgiving Day being the first. Personally I would trade guacamole for cranberry sauce any day. And it does pair well with turkey. But I digress.

The three most popular Super Bowl snacks are chips and dip, chicken wings and pizza. Super Bowl Sunday is a busy day for pizza restaurants, and the National Chicken Council says Americans eat 1.4 billion chicken wings during the game. Holy guacamole, Colonel Sanders!

If that number is correct, and I don't see why the Chicken Council would lie about it, that's enough wings to give every attendee of every Super Bowl since 1967 each 342 wings. Now there's something to crow about.

In the crunch heard across America, four million pounds of pretzels, eight million pounds of popcorn and two million pounds of nuts are consumed during the Super Bowl. It's a wonder anyone can hear the play-by-play.

Add to that twenty-eight million pounds of potato chips, which would make a trail 293,000 miles long if you laid the chips all out end to end, though I'm not sure why you would.

It's all washed down with some 325 million gallons of beer, or enough to fill 493 Olympic-size swimming pools if you drained the water and poured in the suds. Don't though. After spending the afternoon snacking and yelling at the television, a leisurely swim might be just what everyone needs.

Is it any wonder there's a twenty percent increase in antacid sales on the Monday following the Super Bowl and seven million employees call in sick for work? What isn't clear is if they're staying home to mourn a loss or because they overdid it on beer and chicken wings.

Before I go any further I have a disclaimer which a better writer would have put at the top of this essay. I don't know who came up with all of these numbers or how they did it, and the estimates vary widely. But when it comes to the food consumed on Super Bowl Sunday, there is one indisputable statistic: it's a lot.

In fact, I read that the average American puts away some six thousand calories on Super Bowl Sunday. That's two or three days' worth for most of us, and we're not even the ones running up and down the field. Sure, Super Bowl watchers burn some calories cheering, but probably not enough to break even.

At any rate, now I know who's facing off in the upcoming Super Bowl. It's the Americans versus the Scale. I'm betting on the Scale but rooting for the Americans. Go, team!

Love, Honor and Make You See Things My Way

THIS YEAR I'M GOING TO GIVE my Valentine the best gift of all: understanding. And by that, I mean his understanding of me. Instead of a card I'm going to give him this letter explaining why I do the things I do. Try it yourself. I think you'll find it's a nice way to help your partner hear your side without having to listen to theirs.

My Dearest Valentine,

We're blessed to have the same basic attitudes, values and beliefs. Our marriage has lasted these many years because we agree on politics, religion and the generous use of garlic and onions in family meals.

But there are a few smaller issues that have troubled us over the years, and as my gift to you I'm going to take the time now to explain my side of things so you'll know why I'm right. Oh, and happy Valentine's Day.

1. Yes, it's true that I have a peculiar tendency to leave cupboard doors and dresser drawers hanging open, giving the impression that someone just broke in and ransacked the place looking to steal our socks and Tupperware. I know this annoys you but it's such a waste of time to close a door I'm just going to have to open again in a day or two.

    And give me some credit. I do occasionally sashay through the kitchen, closing doors like Vanna White turning letters, usually before we have company or after one of us has a little kneecap mishap. And there was the day I read that I could add fullness to my hair by spraying it with hairspray then quickly bending at the waist and tossing my head. Unfortunately the article didn't mention I should close all our cupboard doors first.

    Anyway, I'm hurt you haven't noticed that I've been doing things your way more since we got the cat and I realized that someone who uses a litter box could be running though our casserole dishes.

2. I know you think I'm never ready when we're going out. But really? Me, late for anything? You'll recall I even had our son on my due date. Never mind that my due date was April Fools' Day.

    If anyone is causing us to be late, it's you. Remember last Friday night? You asked if I was ready and I said, "Absolutely. Let's go." But then you went off to find your glasses. Someone who doesn't have time to close a cupboard door certainly doesn't have time to stand around waiting for you to find your glasses, so while I waited I started loading the dishwasher. You found your glasses, then looked through the mail while you waited for me to finish. I finished with the dishwasher and saw you reading the mail, so I started sorting the laundry. You finished with the mail, sat down on the couch to wait, sighed and took out your cell-phone. And that, Valentine, is why we missed the movie—because you were staring at your phone.

3. I admit it. Over the years, I've given away and, yes, even thrown away a few things you wish we'd kept. Honestly though, I've never knowingly disposed of something you really cared about— not while you were looking anyway.

    In many marriages, including ours, there's a collector and there's a disposer, and if there isn't a disposer there should be. Collectors keep everything because they either love it or they think they might need it someday. Disposers can't imagine why anyone would need or love an old license plate or a pen that doesn't write. In our marriage you're the collector and I'm the disposer. It's true that if we were both dispos-ers, we might not always have the exact doohickey or thingamajig we need. But if we were both collectors we wouldn't be able to find it anyway.

4. It must be annoying how I order healthful meals then snitch your less-than-healthy food off your plate. But if it bothers you so much you could start ordering more wholesome food yourself. I promise I'll never steal a carrot stick off your plate. Anyway, I'm only thinking of you. You shouldn't eat all those French fries by yourself.

And speaking of healthy eating, you know how, when I send you to the grocery store for fruit, low fat milk and whole grain bread, you come home with chips and ice cream too? Don't let the fact that I devour them make you think I want you to keep doing that. You know me. I eat ice cream for the same reason George Mallory said he climbed Mount Everest: Because it's there. Also because I like it. And it's safer than mountain climbing.

5.   I know you think I worry too much but you should be glad I do. Worry works. Think back to how many times I worried that I was going to burn the house down because I thought I forgot to unplug my curling iron. I never burned the house down, did I? Never mind that I also I never left my curling iron on.

But think of all the bad things I didn't have the good sense to worry about that *have* happened. I wasn't worrying when I got food poisoning on our vacation. I wasn't worrying when the airline lost our luggage. And I wasn't worrying that year our tire went flat, our oven died, and our printer stopped printing—all just before Christmas. Or, at least, I wasn't worrying about any of those things when they happened. I now try to worry about them a little each day, and none of them have happened since. You're welcome.

Valentine Verses

STRUGGLING TO SAY JUST THE RIGHT THING to your sweetheart this Valentine's Day? Try one of the following clever, sentimental verses I've come up with. Just select the verse that fits your relationship and copy it onto a heart-shaped piece of red construction paper. Use more than one verse—if you think your relationship can take it.

Your spouse is sure to treasure your simple homemade card as much as any gift, but to be on the safe side, you might want to give one of those too.

Verses for Your Valentine

Darling,
Love is a mystery! And so is the reason you put empty cereal boxes back in the cupboard.

Sugar Dumpling,
No, that outfit doesn't make you look fat. Nothing could make you look fat. Now don't ask me again.

To my very fit spouse,
From this Valentine's Day forward, I promise to go the extra mile in our relationship if you will go the extra foot. That's all it would take for you to carry your dirty dishes from the sink to the dishwasher.

My Fashionably Late Love,
You look fine. The house looks fine. Now could we go already?

Sweetheart,
I'm so glad that we never let little things like whether the seat is up or down spoil our bliss. But if you forget to reload the toilet paper dispenser one more time you can start going next door to use the bathroom.

Beloved,
I promise to stop talking when you're reading the news on your phone—if you promise to stop reading it at the dinner table.

My Fascinating Valentine,
I love to listen when you talk. And talk and talk.

To My Big Strong Husband,
If anyone is tough enough to lift his dirty clothes off the floor and toss them into the hamper, it's you.

Dear,
You're right—as usual.

Cuddle Bug,
I promise to stop elbowing you in the ribs when you snore—
if you promise to stop snoring.

Oh, Baby,
You're hot! But I'm freezing. Touch that thermostat again
and I'll trade you in for an electric blanket.

Cool Valentine,
No, I don't think it's chilly in here. But I do think you look
wonderful in wool.

Sweetie Pie!
We make such a cute couple. I bet we'd look great in a
duplex!

My Altruistic Valentine,
I admire your generosity. I just wish you'd stop giving my
stuff away.

My Sentimental Valentine,
It's so cute how you get attached to your belongings. But
shouldn't you give your old clothes to someone who can
fit into them?

Love of My Life,
After all the wonderful years we've had together, I feel like
I can almost read your mind. Now if I could just read your
handwriting in the checkbook.

My Love,
Of course I agree that our home should be clean. But I'd rather my vehicle be clean.

To My Favorite Traveling Chum,
How I value your wisdom and support—except when I'm driving.

To My Companion on Life's Highway,
Yes, I think you're a good driver. And with some coaching from me you could be a *great* driver.

Dearest,
You make me gloriously happy—some of the time.

My Cute Little Couch Potato,
I could sit and stare at you cuddled up in front of the television all day but one of us has to do the laundry.

Happy Valentine's Day, Honey!
See, I do not always forget!

Ode to an Extra Day

YOU REMEMBER that old poem?

> *Thirty days hath September,*
> *April, June and November*
> *All the rest have thirty-one,*
> *Excepting February alone*
> *And that has twenty-eight days clear*
> *And twenty-nine in each leap year*

In honor of leap year, I'd like to revise it a bit:

> *This ditty's stood the test of time,*
> *Though 'alone' and 'one' don't even rhyme.*
> *And February, feeling left out*
> *Every four years gets a little more clout.*

An extra day, but I'd like to know
Why put it in a month with snow?
And another thing: what's the reason
We add it during campaign season?

Leap day wasn't actually created to give presidential candidates one more day to campaign, but that is one of its drawbacks. We actually have it because the solar year, the time required for the sun to make one complete cycle of the seasons, is 365 days, five hours, forty-eight minutes and forty-six seconds. In other words we start every year almost six hours too early because no one wants to stay up until 6 a.m. to see in the new year.

Without leap day to make up for it, we'd be a full twenty-four days ahead of the seasons a hundred years from now. We wouldn't even have our leaves raked and the calendar would be calling for snow shovels—just like now.

The Roman dictator Julius Caesar, who is considered the father of leap year, added an extra day to keep the calendar year synchronized with the seasons. I imagine he was trying to save snowbirds from leaving Arizona during the spring blizzards up north. How thoughtful. No wonder they named a salad after him.

I'm kidding. That was a different Caesar. And Julius didn't have it quite right anyway. Five hours, forty-eight minutes and forty-six seconds multiplied by four equals... well, I don't know what it equals, but it doesn't equal a full day so further adjustments were necessary. This is too complicated for me to get into, mainly because I don't understand it. Suffice it to say 2100, 2200 and 2300 will not be leap years, even though they're divisible by four. Lucky!

No extra day of campaigning for presidential candidates.

An astronomer named Aloysius Lilius came up with our modern calendar. He was so accurate that whoever's responsible for such things these days only has to add a leap second to the clock every few years and I'm glad they do it. I always appreciate the extra sleep.

Unfortunately Mr. Lilius died in 1576, six years before Pope Gregory XIII officially introduced his calendar, which may be why it's called the Gregorian calendar and not the Liliusian calendar. That doesn't seem fair to Lilius. Maybe we should name a salad after *him*.

Anyway, he's long gone, and I want to know who's responsible for making sure those extra days and seconds keep getting added because I have some suggestions for them.

For starters, if you're going to add an extra day to the calendar, why do it during an election year? And in February? Nobody wants more February except ski resort operators and people in the southern hemisphere.

And another thing. According to my extensive research, February 29 occurs on Mondays and Wednesdays more often than on other days. What kind of person arranges the calendar to have more Mondays? I'd like my extra days, and for that matter my extra seconds, on Saturdays in the spring and not during election years.

Still, I look forward to February 29 every four years though I realize not everyone does. Some superstitious types think the whole year is cursed and that we'd be wise to put off weddings, new jobs and large purchases until it's over. But I think their luck would go downhill fast if they told their new boss they couldn't start until the following year.

And if everyone avoided home and car purchases every four years, leap years would be terribly unlucky for realtors and car dealers.

Some people think February 29 is a terrible day for a birthday too, but I disagree. I'd go so far as to say people who have birthdays on Leap Day are special. You have a one in 1,461 chance of being born a leapling, as they're called. Also, leapster or leaper, not to be confused with leper which is something else entirely and it's not lucky at all.

Less than .07 percent of the world's population were born on leap day which makes them rare and exotic, like white buffalo, blue moons and affordable health insurance.

Personally I love leap day. It's a perfect day for putting my old photos into albums, organizing the filing cabinet and cleaning that layer of greasy dust off the top of my kitchen cupboards. Those are the kinds of things I never get done in 365 days. And if I don't get them done on leap day, they're the kinds of things I can put off for another four years.

Still, I realize that an extra day isn't helpful for everyone so I'd like to dedicate the final verse of my updated poem to those who don't benefit from it.

It's no help to have an added day
For salaried workers with no extra pay,
Prisoners spending leap year in jail,
And all the candidates who'll fail.

The Times, They Are A-Changin'

IMAGINE YOU AND YOUR FAMILY walk into a crowded church service on a sunny March morning and everyone turns to look at you. Then they all start singing—the closing hymn. Obviously they remembered what you did not: to set the clocks ahead the night before.

My advice is to act casual. Maybe they'll think you're returning from a quick trip to the restroom—with your whole family.

And don't be too hard on yourself. You won't be alone. Similar scenes will be playing out across the country on Sunday and probably Monday too. It happens whenever we spring ahead, which, by the way, makes it sound a lot more fun than it is.

Everyone knows you can't fool Mother Nature. But we keep trying to trick Father Time and it's clear it ticks him off. Sorry. Research does suggest that Daylight Saving Time contributes to health problems, motor vehicle accidents and heated arguments over whether it's Daylight *Savings* or Daylight *Saving* Time. Before your family comes to blows over that let me assure you it's *saving*. I read it on the internet so it must be right.

Whatever you call it, a lot of people blame Ben Franklin for it. But it wasn't his fault. The first person to suggest adjusting the clocks was actually New Zealand entomologist George Vernon Hudson. In 1895, he proposed advancing them two full hours in the summer because he wanted more daylight for hunting insects. Thankfully Hudson's proposal didn't...uh...fly.

Two hours! Can you imagine? People would be dozing off on their way to work Monday morning instead of waiting until they got there to do it.

In 1907, an Englishman named William Willett proposed advancing the clocks twenty minutes every Sunday in April, then reversing them twenty minutes per week in September. I'm glad no one listened to him either. I'd never know what time it is.

The Germans were the first to institute Daylight Saving Time in 1916 and the United States followed suit in 1918 as a wartime measure, though I don't see how it would help in a war. Everyone would be too tired to fight. Maybe that's why it was repealed in 1919.

It returned for good in 1966 and we've been stuck with it ever since. It's not all bad. Mostly, but not all. Just think, if we didn't have to get up an hour earlier the second Sunday in March we wouldn't get to sleep an hour later on the first Sunday in November.

Plus the creators of Daylight Saving Time had the good sense to schedule it for a Sunday rather than a

Monday morning. Pastors are probably more forgiving than employers are.

Whether or not Daylight Saving Time saves energy is disputed but I know for a fact it doesn't save *my* energy. For me, it's like jet lag without a trip. And I'm not alone. The Monday after Daylight Saving Time begins has been dubbed "Sleepy Monday" and for good reason. It will never be a national holiday. We're all too tired to celebrate.

In fact, research shows that in the week after we spring ahead there's an increase in cyber loafing—employees wasting time on the internet—because they're tired. Or at least that's the excuse they give if you catch them doing it. And saying you're too tired to work does sound better than saying you were shopping for fishing gear online.

Not only is everybody tired, some of us are just plain befuddled by the time change ritual. Many years ago my family took our Japanese exchange student with us as we went to visit relatives that particular weekend in the spring. On Friday she didn't question us when we told her to set her watch ahead as we traveled east from Mountain Time to Central Time. But they don't play with their clocks where she comes from, so she was puzzled on Saturday night when we told her to set her clock ahead again because Daylight Saving Time would begin overnight. Then the next day, as we headed back into Mountain Time, she was not only confused, she was annoyed. In a tone I'd never heard her use during her otherwise pleasant stay with us, she said, "Just tell me what time is it where we are right now."

Once when my son was young we held his birthday party on the Sunday Daylight Saving Time began. One guest's parents forgot about the time change and showed up an hour late. Lucky we still had cake and ice cream.

Another guest's parents thought it was time to "fall back" an hour. They brought their child two hours late, just as the party was breaking up. We had no cake, no ice cream and not much else either. My son still got the gift though.

It can be confusing, and it was important that I understood it because I brought the birthday boy. That's why long ago I came up with a clever way to remember which way to set your clocks: In the spring, you spring out of your bed because you're an hour late for work. In the fall, you fall back into it when you realize you're not.

A Chance of Madness
in March

I'M ALWAYS A DAY LATE AND A DOLLAR SHORT. And in this case I'm many years late and a billion dollars short. You may have heard that back in 2014 Warren Buffet offered a billion-dollar March Madness prize to anyone who could successfully pick all sixty-four team brackets in the NCAA men's basketball tournament. You can't win if you don't play, and I didn't play...or win. Of course, sometimes you can't win even if you do play, as everyone who played found out.

Estimates vary but some mathematicians say your chance of picking all the tournament brackets correctly is one in 9.2 quintillion. That's a nine with eighteen zeroes. Put another way, Warren Buffet had nothing to worry about.

March Madness "grips the national sports psyche from the second week of March through the first week of April," or so I read on a sports website. No offense, sports fans, but many things grip my psyche during March but basketball isn't one of them. I sure wouldn't spend a lot of time guessing tournament brackets when I have a better chance of winning the lottery and being struck by lightning, which would really take the fun out of winning the lottery.

My chances of choosing all the brackets would probably be even worse since I don't even follow the sport. The last basketball game I watched was between the Harding County Ranchers girls' basketball team and a team I can't recall even though I had a bird's eye view of the action—from the bench.

I'm not even sure what tournament fans mean by "bracket." In my world a bracket is a seldom-used punctuation mark or the doohickey that holds a shelf on the wall, either of which can drive me mad in the right circumstances.

Here's what I know after consulting the well of sports knowledge, the internet: March Madness refers to the National Collegiate Athletic Association Men's and Women's Basketball Tournaments which decide the national champions of college basketball. I can see how that would get you all worked up if your psyche is gripped by that sort of thing.

But if I'm going to go mad in March, and there's a better than one in 9.2 quintillion chance that I will, I can't blame basketball.

I go a little mad every time I want to return something and can't figure out how to fit it back in the box it came in. Or when my cling wrap clings to itself instead of the bowl. Or when I think I smell fresh-baked cookies and find out it's one of those cheater cookie-scented candles.

But those things drive me mad year-round. March may have more than its share of crazy makers. How about getting pinched because you didn't wear green on St. Patrick's Day, or having to set the clock ahead or calling something corned beef when there's no corn involved? And what about Pi Day on March 14? Pie grips my psyche, even when it's spelled wrong.

The Ides of March, March 15, corresponds to the date on the Roman calendar when Julius Caesar was assassinated in 44 BC. I think that was followed by a bit of madness, but I haven't read Shakespeare's *Julius Caesar* since I was forced to in college and my memory of 44 BC is a little rusty, as anything from 44 BC would be by now.

There's national If Pets Had Thumbs Day on March 3 and Extraterrestrial Abductions Day on March 20. If anything could grip a psyche, I think it would be space aliens and poodles with thumbs.

Fortunately, if we non-sports fans make it to March 30, we can celebrate I Am in Control Day which will be refreshing after a month of madness. We may have a slight relapse on April Fools' Day but then we'll return to normal, whatever that is for us. Meanwhile the psyches of basketball fans will still be gripped for a few more days.

And the Oscar Goes To...

AMAZING! That handsome fella just jumped off a speeding train onto the back of a galloping horse at the very moment the train exploded, spewing fire and debris far and wide. But that's not the amazing part. He had one leg in a cast, he was carrying the wounded train engineer on his back and he was being pursued by masked bandits. But that's not the amazing part either. What's truly incredible is that he won't even win an Academy Award for Best Stunt, and not just because I made the whole thing up.

The truth is, there isn't an Academy Award for Best Stunt, at least as of this writing. I've never sat through the entire Academy Awards program and I probably won't this year either, but I do love movies. And if I were running the show, there would definitely be an award for best stunt. And if the show weren't already eighteen hours long, I'd add a few other awards too:

1. **The Award for Not Busting out Laughing When You Have to Say Dumb Stuff:** I admit I say dumb stuff sometimes and I don't usually laugh when I do it. But I don't think I could keep a straight face if I had to say, "Go ahead. Make my day," or "It was beauty killed the beast," or "I'll get you, my pretty, and your little dog, too!" Oh, wait. The Wicked Witch of the West did laugh, didn't she? Maybe that's why she didn't win an Oscar.

2. **The Award for Kissing People You Don't Even Like:** I don't follow Hollywood gossip, but as much kissing as goes on in the movies, I have to believe that occasionally actors are called on to lock lips with someone they'd rather kick in the shins. And they have to do it enthusiastically on camera with a set full of onlookers, knowing the whole world will see it and their significant other is likely to ask them about it later.

3. **The Award for Most Convincing Death Scene:** Next to kissing people they don't like, I think death must be the hardest scene for actors to pull off believably since one can assume most of them haven't had actual experience. And those who have aren't talking about it.

4. **The Award for Most Humiliating Grovel:** Actors frequently grovel, especially in romantic comedies. Often close to the end of the movie the handsome leading man—and it usually is the leading man—makes a dramatic entrance, takes the blame for everything that's gone wrong in the relationship, begs forgiveness and pledges his undying love,

sometimes in front of a group of the leading lady's friends. I've never heard of a man doing this in real life, though I've often wished they would. It's a talent and it should be rewarded. Plus, as a woman I'd like to encourage that kind of behavior in men.

5. **The Award for Most Believable Water Works:** Actors are often required to snivel, blubber and bawl convincingly. I'm one of those people who tears up watching greeting card commercials. But I'm afraid the only way I could sob on set is if the director yelled at me. I know I could be convincing in that role, but I'd probably also forget my lines.

6. **The Award for Having the Good Sense to Wear Comfortable Shoes:** In the movies you regularly see women wearing high heels while they play everything from spies to cat burglars to police officers. I caught a few minutes of a crime show the other night. There was a beautiful villain, stylishly dressed and holding a gun to some guy's ribs. Unfortunately, because of her high heels, she couldn't walk heel to toe like less stylish villains do. Instead, she took quick, bouncy little steps, like a needle on a sewing machine as she escorted him from the room. In real life he could have just tipped her over and escaped because he'd had the foresight to wear comfortable shoes.

In my opinion it isn't just silly, it's downright dangerous for active women to wear dumb girl shoes in action movies. But then maybe they use stunt doubles, in which case there really ought to be an award for that.

Party on During National Spring Cleaning Week

WELL, DANG! I've just learned that the fourth Sunday of March kicked off National Spring Cleaning Week, seven glorious days set aside to celebrate our instinct to clean, and I missed it. Maybe because I don't have an instinct to clean.

I'm not sure why anyone would celebrate cleaning anyway, spring or otherwise. And even if it is worth celebrating, I think a full week is excessive. We only get one day to celebrate far more important things like independence and my birthday. Plus I don't think it's fair that No Housework Day only gets April 7, though I've been known to observe it for several months at a time.

Nevertheless, I apologize for not letting you know sooner. I realize I've left you with a difficult decision to make. You could go ahead and do your spring cleaning in April. I don't recommend that. You could put it off until next March and blame me. I don't recommend that either since National Blame Someone Else Day isn't until the first Friday the 13th of the year. Or you could skip spring cleaning altogether and just do extensive research on the subject like I've done.

I think you'll find researching spring cleaning is much more enjoyable than doing it. If you do an internet search of spring cleaning, you'll find that there are at least 665 million results. Take the time to read them all and you won't have time to do any cleaning for the next twelve years. Clearly I'm not the only one who would rather write about it than do it.

I didn't read all 665 million articles, but I did stumble on a startling statistic in one of them. According to an organization called the American Cleaning Institute, *ninety-one percent of Americans engage in spring cleaning—or say they do, though I don't recall anyone asking me.*

And a whopping seventy-six percent of the population claim they do it every year. Wow! I had no idea that many Americans could agree on anything, especially something so controversial.

The Institute, which represents producers of cleaning products, claims that *only six percent of the population admit they never do any spring cleaning. That either means I'm part of a very elite group or that a lot of people lie to the* American Cleaning Institute.

I also noticed some common elements in articles about spring cleaning. A lot of writers use words like "easy" and "a breeze" to describe it. Some even go so far as to say, "Spring cleaning can be fun!" Those are people who need more hobbies.

Also, if there's a photo in an article about spring cleaning, it will be of a smiling, attractive woman looking like she enjoys National Spring Cleaning Week even more than Chocolate Éclair Day, June 22. Readers are smart enough to know that the reason she's smiling is because she's a well-paid model with a housecleaning service.

Observant readers will also note that she has no dirt on her hands, no smudges on her face and no cobwebs in her neatly coiffed hair. It's obvious her house was clean before she took out the broom. I'd smile too.

Most of the articles offered helpful tips. And I did think one author's toilet-cleaning tip was very clever: drop two denture-cleaning tablets into the bowl and let sit overnight. In the morning, brush then floss...I mean flush.

There was also a lot of talk of white vinegar in these articles. I realize that when you use white vinegar your home smells like you do your own pickling, which is bound to impress your guests. However, no one will believe you've been pickling before the cucumbers have even sprouted so I'd hold off with the vinegar until fall.

Finally, you'll notice that if you were to do everything the articles suggest—from reorganizing your spice rack to resealing your grout to cleaning out your gutters--it would take a lot longer than one week. What are they thinking? National Clean Out Your Closets Month alone takes up the entire month of January.

Before you do anything rash, consider this. Spring cleaning time may be a good time to clean the oven, clean your refrigerator and polish the silver. But keep in mind that if you never use your oven, you'll never have to clean your oven. If you have no silver, you'll never have to polish it. And a refrigerator doesn't require cleaning if you use it as I do, just to keep water cold.

Rather than spending all the time it would take to clean your house from top to bottom, I believe it would be far more efficient to build a new one. I'm kidding! But if you really must clean I suggest you spread it out rather than jamming it all into one week. Spend a few minutes one day and half an hour another day, say on April 3 and June 14.

I'm not the only one who thinks this is a better idea. Someone has declared Clean Off Your Desk Day the second Monday of January, Clean Out Your Garage Day the Saturday after Labor Day and Clean Out Your Refrigerator Day November 15, probably so we can toss last Thanksgiving's leftovers in time to make room for this year's.

Besides National Spring Cleaning Week has come and gone. And I feel terrible that I didn't alert you in time to observe it appropriately. If you still feel like celebrating you could always come over to my house. And bring a mop.

I'm only half kidding. The author of one article I read actually suggested getting motivated for spring cleaning by scheduling a big party for the weekend following your cleaning blitz. I'll say this as tactfully as I can—what a dumb idea.

Why would you clean your house then invite a truckload of guests over to track in dirt? I'd rather have a party *before* I do any spring-cleaning. I'd make it a theme party with the theme, of course, being spring cleaning and I'd ask my guests to bring brooms and dust rags. If *seventy-six* percent of Americans are willing to clean house this spring, some of them might as well be cleaning mine.

In like a Lion and Out like a Practical Joke

IT'S A BEAUTIFUL SPRING MORNING and a coworker shows up at work with a box of doughnuts to celebrate. Well, isn't that nice! You take a big bite out of one and discover it's filled. You love filled doughnuts—except when they're filled with mayonnaise. April fool!

Whose idea was it to dedicate an entire day to practical jokes anyway? Why devote a whole day to bad behavior? We already have a holiday for that. It's called New Year's Eve.

Some blame the Romans. Some blame the Celts. Some blame the adoption of the Gregorian calendar and the ensuing change of the New Year. But I think April Fools' pranks have been around as long as April has been around—even as long as seasons have been around. Spring weather is Mother Nature's equivalent of pouring a bag of Skittles into a bowl of M&M'S, and that's illegal in most states.

After a long cold winter, you walk outside one beautiful morning and say, "Spring is finally here." And the next day you slip on freezing rain, break your leg and wind up in a cast until September. April fool! That's how spring is. It's here! No, it's not. Yes, it is. No, it's not. March is in like a lion and out like a lamb. Then the big mean lion comes back and chases the cute little lamb around until the poor thing decides to stay with friends in Arizona for a few weeks.

Spring has been making fools of human beings—and lambs—since time began, and humans have followed her lead. Thankfully most of us confine our tricks to one day. Civilization couldn't survive an entire season of mayonnaise in our doughnuts and thumbtacks on our office chairs.

I've endured a few April Fools' Day pranks in my life. There was the fake fire alarm that got me out of the shower with the shampoo still in my hair. And there was the false claim that I had a flat tire, which caused me to run out to the parking lot to check while everyone inside laughed at me. At least I was wearing more than a bathrobe for that one. I retaliated by telling the prankster she had spinach in her teeth. She might have fallen for it too, were it not for the fact that she hadn't eaten spinach in a good long while. It was the best I could do on short notice.

Spring weather has played far worse tricks on me. There are springs I'm forced to use my umbrella and my snow shovel in the same week, run my air conditioner and my heater on the same day and eat ice cream and soup in the same meal.

In the spring a young man's fancy lightly turns to thoughts of love, or so poet Alfred, Lord Tennyson said. As a middle-aged woman, my fancy lightly turns to thoughts of spring cleaning. April fool! I never think about that.

Actually my fancy lightly turns to thoughts of lower heating bills, which isn't nearly as poetic.

Despite it all, spring is still my favorite season—except in the fall when fall is my favorite season. And autumn has one big advantage over spring. There's no October Fools' Day.

A Chocolate a Day Keeps the Doctor Away

I'M GOING TO USE A FIVE-GALLON TUB for my Easter basket this year, and it won't be filled with hardboiled eggs and Easter grass either. I'm going to pack it to the brim with chocolate eggs, bunnies and bars because I just read yet another article touting the health benefits of chocolate. That's why I eat it; it's good for me.

The article summarized a review published in the *European Journal of Preventive Cardiology* which found that eating chocolate more than once per week was linked with a reduced risk of coronary artery disease. Healthy heart, big butt. I think it's worth it.

But wait! Maybe we can have our chocolate cake and eat it too. Another article I read said chocolate is actually associated with lower body mass index or BMI. I'm not making that up (though it does sound like the kind of thing I would make up).

Researchers at the University of California surveyed more than a thousand people about their weekly food intake. Those who reported less frequent chocolate consumption were heavier than those who reported eating chocolate more often. Now there's news you can use. And I do.

I've also heard that indulging in chocolate daily makes you better looking, more creative and just plain smarter. Okay, I did make that up. But it isn't hard to find articles about the benefits of chocolate. People are hungry for this kind of health information. We just eat it up. I know I do. In fact, sometimes I go overboard. When I read that eating oily fish is good for your heart, I went right out and bought a crate of kipper snacks. No, I didn't do that. But I do follow good health advice when I hear it—if I like it.

You might wonder what my body mass index is after heeding so much good advice. Well, BMI is determined by dividing your weight in pounds by your height in inches squared and multiplying by a conversion factor of 703. In other words, it's none of your business.

Let's just say it would be a lot higher if I weren't a bit of a skeptic. When I stumble across a story about how good chocolate is for me, my first question is always who paid for the study? Ghirardelli? Hershey's? Mars, Incorporated? And did that affect the results? I'm cynical by nature, plus I want to write and thank them.

I'm also curious how the data was collected. I'm dubious of studies that rely on participants to report accurately and honestly on their consumption habits. I know I'd be tempted to…uh…fudge my numbers a little.

Also, I want to know exactly how much chocolate it takes to stop hair loss, make you more charming or whatever other benefit researchers are claiming at the moment. They aren't always clear on this, and I think it's important that we have some guidance. Chocolate Easter eggs are harder to limit than other health foods. You never hear of anyone overdoing it on kale. No one eats so many skinless chicken breasts that they can no longer waddle. I'm fond of arugula, but I don't polish off the whole bag every time I have one in the house. And while chocolate might be good for me, it might not be good for me in the quantity I like. Even arugula wouldn't be healthful in that quantity.

Some studies linking chocolate consumption to good health say all you need to benefit is a square a day. But a square what? A square foot?

Others say as little as four grams a day is all it takes. The only grams I'm familiar with are graham crackers, and I don't think that's the same thing. So I went to that great treasure trove of diet advice in the sky, the internet, where I learned that one gram is roughly equal to four small paper-clips. That wasn't helpful. Nobody eats those.

So in the interest of science, I went out and bought myself a Hershey bar. I was shocked to see on the label that my itsy-bitsy candy bar weighed forty-three grams or the equivalent of 172 paperclips. If I were to eat just four grams a day, it would take me eleven days to eat my little candy bar and on the last day, I'd be forced to eat a Hershey kiss too—or four paperclips.

It seems to me anyone who can eat just four grams of chocolate and leave the rest for another day is not a chocolate lover at all and should relinquish all their Easter candy to me.

Another question I have when I'm reading articles about the health advantages of chocolate is this: Does it really have to be dark chocolate, as a lot of research claims? I do like dark chocolate; I just like it better with milk in it. And sugar—and nuts, toffee or malted milk. Let's say you give me a variety bag of those fun size candy bars this Easter, which would be a nice gesture on your part. Of course, you'd save me time if you gave me a couple of full-sized candy bars instead since I'm just going to unwrap ten or fifteen of the miniatures and eat them all at once anyway. An ounce of chocolate isn't fun; a pound is fun.

At any rate, if you do give me a variety bag of fun size chocolate, here's what will happen: First I'll eat all the milk chocolate with nuts. Then I'll eat all the milk chocolate with toffee or crisped rice or whatever else. Then I'll eat the plain milk chocolate. And finally, after every bit of milk chocolate is gone, I'll eat the dark chocolate—after smearing it with peanut butter.

Which leads me to the final question I have for chocolate researchers. Are the benefits of chocolate enhanced or diminished by all the goodies that go into it? Chocolate is rarely a solo act. It pairs well with malted milk, marshmallows, cookie wafers, and any number of other foods that aren't normally considered healthful. I even tried chocolate-covered bacon once. As it turns out, covering bacon with chocolate amounts to taking two things I like a great deal and turning them into one thing I don't like at all.

And I can't help but think that eating chocolate on bacon—or nougat, or a donut, or a large sundae with caramel, whipped cream and sprinkles—might wipe out some of the health benefits. But I bet you still get to be smarter, better looking and more creative.

Happy Guilt Day

MOMS, IF YOU EVER FEEL LIKE USING GUILT as a parenting tool, I've got just the thing. Put your hand to your heart, sniffle a little and say to your child: "A woman named Anna Jarvis was so devoted to her mom that back in 1908 she actually proposed a national holiday for mothers. And you can't even put your dishes in the dishwasher for me." Sniff, sniff.

We do have Anna Jarvis to thank for Mother's Day—well, Anna and the retailers who assumed rightly that there would be a good profit in it. Then in 1914 President Woodrow Wilson approved a resolution making the second Sunday in May a holiday in honor of what he called "that tender, gentle army, the mothers of America." As a soldier in that tender, gentle army, I am grateful.

Father's Day was also the brainchild of a daughter, so fathers can use guilt just as effectively. In other words, not very. But it was thanks to Sonora Smart Dodd that Washington

State celebrated the nation's first Father's Day on June 19, 1910. Unfortunately, Father's Day was not met with the same enthusiasm that Mother's Day had received. Apparently one florist even claimed that dads don't have the same "sentimental appeal" that mothers have. Ouch! But I think that's just florist-speak for "no one will buy flowers for dads."

Dads didn't help their cause either. One historian wrote that many men scoffed at what they saw as an attempt to "domesticate manliness with flowers and gift-giving...." Many also derided Father's Day as a gimmick to sell gift items men would probably wind up paying for themselves.

It wasn't until 1972, in the middle of his re-election campaign, that Richard Nixon signed a proclamation making Father's Day a federal holiday. Maybe he was courting the dad vote.

At any rate, that was fifty-eight years after Mother's Day became official and it's been playing catch up ever since. There's one measurement that shows just how far it has to go: spending on gifts.

By some reports Americans spend ten billion dollars more on Mother's Day gifts than they do on Father's Day. Maybe it's because Mother's Day comes first. When you spend thirty billion dollars in May you're bound to be a little short on cash come June.

But after a great deal of research, I've decided there's another reason spending on Father's Day gifts lags behind Mother's Day: Father's Day gifts are...how can I say this diplomatically...too dumb to buy. At least the ones I can afford are. Many of the things my husband wants would require him to cosign a loan and that would take the surprise out of gift giving.

I went to that the great gift guide in the sky, the internet, to research Father's Day gifts that don't require taking out a loan. I was worried the whole time that my husband would walk in, see my computer screen and think he was getting a leather beer holster or a toilet bowl mug for his big day. Yup. Those are the kinds of gifts that are out there for dads. And if he wants either of one of those, he's going to have to buy it himself.

Cuff links are also touted as great gifts for dads. Among many others, you can get cuff links that look like tiny circuit boards, the inside of a clock, Rubik's Cubes, gear shifters and brass forty-caliber bullet casings. I can't remember the last time my husband wore a shirt that required cufflinks but if he ever does, I just can't see him accessorizing with bullet casings.

Grilling equipment is another common dad gift and my husband does enjoy grilling, mainly because it involves fire. But I feel like giving him a grill cleaning brush for Father's Day is a bit like giving me a broom for Mother's Day.

You also find plenty of alcohol and alcohol accessories when you go searching for Dad's Day gifts. There are monogrammed whiskey glasses, beer making kits, cocktail sets for business travel and even Scotch-infused toothpicks, the implication being that we're all driving dad to drink.

The cliché of a Father's Day gift is the necktie, and there are many to choose from. I saw a tie that looks like an eyechart, which would be great for a father who's an optometrist. Another one looked like piano keys, which would be swell for a dad who's a musician. And I found one covered with lipstick kisses. I have no idea what kind of dad that would be good for.

When my husband was an elementary school principal he had a closet full of goofy ties he wore especially for his students. But I think even he would draw the line at a necktie that looks like a giant strip of raw bacon.

And the bacon theme is big for Father's Day gift giving and not just for ties. Along with ties, there are bacon-scented candles, soap and even shaving cream all of which you can wrap in bacon-scented wrapping paper. Talk about dads using guilt against their children. "Mom gets flowers, jewelry and gift certificates for massages. I get bacon I can't even eat."

Blubbering about Graduation

Dear graduate!

You may not believe this, but a few years ago I gave the valedictorian's address at my high school graduation. It only seems like a long time ago to you because you weren't born yet.

And don't be impressed about the valedictorian honor. There were twenty-eight in my graduating class; even the students with a D average were in the top thirty.

I had planned to regale you with excerpts from my speech but I can't remember a thing about it—lucky for you. In fact I barely remember the night at all except for what I wore: a funny hat and what looked like a bathrobe in my school colors. I do vividly recall getting a lot of money through the mail around that time though. It was a long time ago and I still miss that part.

But the speech is gone from my memory. And I doubt it lives on in anyone else's either. So in lieu of inspirational thoughts from my graduation speech let me just wish you well and ask for your understanding. This is an exciting but difficult time for you. You face important decisions about your future, poignant farewells to your past, and through it all, the blubbering of relatives. Forgive us if we embarrass you. We can't help but be proud of you—or stunned.

But there's much more than that to our shows of emotion. Your parents are understandably overcome with joy—and worry. They're anxious about college funding. They're wondering if they'll ever hear from you again after you leave home—or if you'll ever leave home. And they're not sure you even know how to do your own laundry yet. Don't laugh. What have you done to reassure them?

Besides that, some of your peers have shown some very poor judgment in the last weeks of school. Kids who haven't been in trouble since kindergarten were suddenly letting chickens loose in algebra class. If your parents started acting like that you'd worry too.

But those of us who are not your parents get teary-eyed too. Seeing the graduation of someone we once played peek-a-boo with leaves us feeling sentimental. Also old.

You'll feel the same way in a few short years. And that is, I suppose, our biggest problem. "A few short years" ago is all it seems. One minute we were crossing the stage, our biggest concern whether our diploma was signed; the next we've got a mortgage, bifocals and a muffin top. There you are with your whole life ahead of you, and here we are facing down a mid-life crisis—or worse. The world is your oyster; we've become old crabs.

I suppose that explains why we keep offering you advice which, by the way, you should at least pretend to listen to.

We've learned a few things since we were your age. Plus we just gave you that cash for graduation. You owe us something.

Where we are in our own lives also explains why we keep asking you what you plan to do now. It's not that we're nosey. Well, some of us are nosey. But mainly what we are is jealous. Your graduation causes us to look back at what we've accomplished since we celebrated our own. This can be painful since for many of us, it isn't much. Let that be a lesson to you. If you're not careful you could wind up like us.

Still, I realize all those questions about your future can be annoying, especially if you have no idea what you want to be yet. Don't worry; there's a good chance the adults in your life still don't know that either.

Whatever you decide to do though, do it well. You'll be taking care of us in our old age, you know. Plus we've really botched things up. Just look at global warming. And congress. We need you to do a better job than we have. But remember part of being better is never telling us that you are.

As if all of that isn't enough, graduations themselves can be downright tedious. At the most recent one I attended, a university graduation with hundreds of graduates, I saw a man reading a newspaper. I didn't blame him. In fact I desperately wanted to ask him for the lifestyle page.

It doesn't help that by spring graduation time the weather has warmed and with it the gymnasiums. Your friends and relatives sit fanning themselves in a room where, not so long ago, we were watching a band concert or a real nail-biter of a basketball game. Now we're all gussied up and climbing onto bleachers that were meant to be climbed on only in sneakers and jeans.

But then we catch sight of you. You look almost regal, even in that getup. We know why you wear it, of course. The hat is designed for easy stacking during shipping and the gown is intended to cover the shorts and tank top we know you're wearing underneath it.

Still, there's something dignified about you. You're all grown up and ready to take on the world. Everything seems possible for you. We're not even sure we can find our car in the parking lot. You'd blubber too.

This is No Time for Inventors to Rest

I HAVE A LOT IN COMMON with the instrument maker, Johann Christoph Denner. He was born in August of 1655, and I was also born in August, though not in 1655. Denner invented the clarinet, and I *played* the clarinet. And when I practiced there were people who cursed the day both of us were born. But I don't want to talk about that now.

I want to talk about National Inventors Month, which is celebrated every May to acknowledge inventions, inventiveness and inventors like Mr. Denner. Also Levi Strauss who invented blue jeans in the 1800s. I have no idea what people wore on weekends in the 1700s.

And let's not forget Clarence Birdseye who in 1930 patented a method for packaging frozen foods, paving the way for TV dinners. Then there was Philo Farnsworth who, also in 1930, patented the television. Before 1930 couch potatoes had to lie in front of their radios all day eating out of tin cans.

And hats off to William Addis of England, who in 1780 made the first toothbrush using cow bones for the handles and bristles from the necks and shoulders of swine for the brush. No more cavities for Mr. Addis but his breath must have smelled like a barnyard.

Zippers were patented in 1893. Prior to that people went around with their jackets open all the time.

The dishwasher was invented in 1850 but it took another hundred years before the technology became efficient enough for the public to notice. By that time the food was *really* dried on.

I often wonder how we balanced our checkbooks before Quicken. Before cell phones, how did we remind our spouses to pick up milk? Before microwaves, how did we thaw out hamburger in time to make goulash for supper? And how did we heat up the goulash for the next five days?

Inventions like these have made life so much better— though it's hard to fully appreciate the microwave after five days of goulash.

But we do owe a lot to inventors. Modern day inventors deserve to rest and celebrate this month. But come June 1 they need to get back to work. There's still much that needs inventing and I can't do it. I wish I were an inventor but I think I'd need more garage space and a basic understanding of many things I don't currently understand at all. No, I'm strictly an idea person.

And here's one of my better ideas. Someone needs to come up with a sleeping bag stuffer. I can store six thousand books on my e-reader and six hundred thousand pages on my flash drive but I can't fit my sleeping bag back into the sack it came in.

And since hotel guests can't be more thoughtful about my sleep issues, I'd like someone to invent hotel doors that close silently instead of with a bang. In the hotels I stay in it sounds like the guests are mad all the time.

I think someone should create a vending machine with a dollar bill iron attached. I have a recurring nightmare where I'm faint with hunger, clutching a fistful of dollar bills and lying at the foot of a vending machine that won't accept my wrinkled money.

And I've been dreaming of a gizmo that would allow me to remotely change my cellphone from vibrate mode to volume ten ever since I somehow dropped it in the trashcan.

Better yet, someone should invent a universal locator. I could just type in what I'm looking for and it would tell me where to find it, whether it's my car keys, my reading glasses or the lid to my food processor.

And how about a one-click way to respond safely to spammers? I would love to be able to send every spammer who emails me ten thousand messages in return, asking them if their mother knows what they're doing. At the same time I'd like a way to snatch back emails I wish I hadn't sent—especially if I accidentally sent it ten thousand times.

Or maybe what I need is an undo button, like my computer software has, for every other part of my life. (I wish I hadn't said that. Undo. I wish I hadn't done that. Undo.)

I have ice cubes to keep my cold drinks cold. Why can't I have hot cubes to keep my hot drinks hot?

I have a self-cleaning oven. So why can't I have a self-cleaning refrigerator, a self-cleaning closet and a self-cleaning toilet? And how about remote controls for my dust rag, my broom and my toilet brush—unless I get the self-cleaner. The inventor who comes up with that will make millions. Just remember I thought of it first.

Wedding Tips from an Eloper

MY HUSBAND AND I ELOPED, since back when we got married we both already had toasters. There were those who criticized us, saying ours wasn't a real wedding. But it was legal, just small. And it seems to have worked. We've been married more than thirty years. Had I thought that more lavish nuptials would have improved our chances of staying married I'd have insisted we go to greater lengths. But I have yet to see a connection between the extravagance of the wedding and the length of the marriage.

Did you know the average American wedding has 131 guests and costs $30,000? For thirty thousand bucks you ought to get some kind of money-back guarantee. Instead, we'd all be wise to save some of that cash for the second time around. I know couples who are still paying for the wedding while they're going through the divorce. It's a shame to see them fighting for custody of the wedding cake stored in their freezer.

I've been to more wedding showers than a punch bowl and I've seen a lot of dumb things done in the name of starting the couple out right. At one shower several of the guests carefully folded each piece of giftwrap, then handed them to the bride. They told her that lining the dresser drawers in her new home with the wrapping paper would ensure a long and happy marriage. Unfortunately, no one explained this tradition to the groom—or his new girlfriend.

At another shower two normally sane women nearly came to blows over the making of a traditional bow bouquet. Or was it a bow hat? Bouquet! Hat! BOUQUET! HAT! They both had very strong feelings about the importance of this exercise because broken bows supposedly signal how many children the couple will eventually have. Thus far, they've had none—despite the fact that some very nice bows were broken during the struggle.

When it comes to the actual wedding, couples jump out of airplanes together or ride away on Harleys or hot air balloons. I've known couples who wrote their own vows, designed the wedding gown and made their own silk flowers. I was invited to a wedding where the couple's dog scampered down the aisle with the rings attached to his collar. I think they're fighting for custody of the dog now. Nothing seems to help. The statistics are dismal.

Certainly that makes gift giving difficult for those of us attending weddings. Not only must we avoid duplicating what other guests are giving the happy couple; we must avoid duplicating what we gave them the last time. My advice is to choose something functional, like a gift certificate to marriage classes.

It's even harder on brides and grooms. I remind those of you about to embark on that adventure that is marriage, it will not matter if your colors are lemon yellow and corn flower blue or mint and mauve. It will not matter whether you spend your honeymoon in Paris or Pittsburgh. None of these are the determining factor in whether your marriage lasts or not.

What is? I have no idea. I don't feel comfortable offering marriage advice even though I'm still married, at least as of this writing. I do, however, have plenty of advice on wedding planning. You may wonder why you should take wedding advice from someone who eloped. Well you shouldn't, but I'm going to offer it anyway.

I love weddings and not just because of the cake. I've been a maid of honor and a bridesmaid many times. I've also served punch, cut and served wedding cake and worked the guest book on a few occasions. All these experiences come together in my new, free checklist:

Wedding Checklist

Six to twelve months prior to the wedding:
- Announce your engagement to family and friends, thus answering the question they've been asking for months or even years: "Are you ever getting married?" But be warned; shortly after the wedding they'll start asking when you're having kids.
- Discuss with your fiancé the style of wedding you both want. He might want to elope and you may want five attendants each and two hundred guests. This provides you with a perfect opportunity to

practice the communication and negotiation skills you'll need every day of your marriage. Or you could just do it your mother's way.

- Register for gifts. This is the fun part. I don't remember this being an option when I was married all those years ago so I'm thinking about doing it now.

Four to six months out:

- Pick a caterer, baker, florist, photographer and videographer. Oh, and someone to marry if you haven't done that yet.
- Order a wedding gown and start an exercise routine so you can fit into it. Don't worry; no one loses weight like a bride-to-be. No one gains it back like a married woman, but we won't go into that here.
- Pick out the tuxes for the groom and groomsmen and choose your bridesmaid's dresses. But be kind. I once wore a beautiful but backless bridesmaid's gown at a January wedding in Minnesota. Out of spite I kept the couple's gift.

Two to four months out:

- If you plan on writing your own vows, do it now. You'll want to put a lot of thought into this. I don't mean to make you nervous, but *everybody* will be listening.
- Send out invitations. It would be a shame to go to all this work and forget this step.

One month out:
- If you're thinking of backing out, now is a good time. You might still get some of your deposits back.
- If you decide to go ahead, don't forget to head over to the DMV for your marriage license. Oh wait. That's your driver's license.
- Pick up your dress and keep it in a safe place away from pets and small children.

Day of:
- Don't panic, but where are the rings? Who has the rings?
- Be on the lookout for pranks. When the priest asked the couple to kneel at a wedding I attended years ago, everyone seated up front could see that the groom's left shoe had a white HELP painted on the bottom. The right one said ME. These things are funnier at other people's weddings.
- Confirm that the musicians, videographer, photographer, officiant and attendants have arrived. Oh, and the person you're marrying. You'll definitely want them to be there too.

There you have it, my foolproof wedding checklist. Following these steps won't guarantee a long marriage but it will improve your chances of having the perfect wedding. And that could affect how many people attend your next one.

The Wiener Takes It All

IT WAS JULY 4 A FEW YEARS AGO. I was having lunch with my husband in one of those restaurants that has giant TV screens on every wall so that all the diners can watch different games and not have to talk to each other.

The screen I faced featured hot dogs grilling. I was hungry and the dogs looked good. But when the scene changed from grilling hot dogs to eating hot dogs I lost my appetite faster than you can say, "I'll have mustard with that." Actually "eating" doesn't begin to describe what was happening. Several men wearing matching T-shirts were cramming hot dogs down their gullets like pelicans at a fish hatchery.

I had a lot of questions at that moment, the main one being why? Eating is one of life's greatest pleasures. It seems like force feeding yourself hot dogs would make it hard to... uh...relish them. Sorry.

Let me pause here to apologize to anyone who has the wherewithal to make it to the end of this essay. Almost nothing lends itself to bad puns more than hot dogs. Except maybe chickens. And I'll get to those too.

Anyway, $10,000 is why. And a bejeweled mustard-yellow belt and all the hot dogs you can eat. Turns out I was watching Nathan's Famous International Hot Dog Eating Contest which is so famous I'd never heard of it. Apparently it's held annually on the Fourth of July at Coney Island, and thousands of people attend to cheer on behavior they'd find repugnant at their own dinner tables.

Thankfully the contest is mercifully short. Ten minutes and it was all over but the bellyache. And I did bellyache. I told my husband that if the purpose of the contest is to promote hot dogs, it didn't work on me. I said it would be a long time before I could even look at a hot dog again, let alone eat one. And I told him watching people stuff themselves with hot dogs is no way to spend Independence Day, though I imagine stuffing *yourself* with them would be even...wurst.

He said, "nice hit" and clapped for the baseball game on the screen behind me.

Joey "Jaws" Chestnut won the contest after eating seventy-two hot dogs. Miki Sudo won the women's division packing in forty-one dogs while her competitors played ketchup. You are what you eat though, so everyone's a wiener. I'm sorry. I can't stop myself.

I won't be watching to see if Joey "Jaws" or Miki Sudo compete this year but you can if you have the stomach for it. The contest is broadcast by ESPN—you know, the sports channel. That seems odd. Nobody thinks it's sport when I have two pieces of pumpkin pie on Thanksgiving or eat the "sharing size" of peanut M&M'S all by myself.

There's NFL, MLB and now MLE, the Major League Eating Federation. I'm not making that up. The MLE hosts around fifty eating contests every year—tamales in Louisville, oysters in New Orleans and wings in Buffalo, to name a few. Their mission, in part, is to "...publicize and execute eating events in a wide variety of food disciplines." I know "discipline" isn't normally the word that comes to my mind when someone overeats anything, including hot dogs. But let me be frank. I think discipline is exactly what it would take to keep seventy-five of them down until the contest is over.

I shouldn't judge. I engaged in my share of eating competitions with my younger brother when I was growing up, including one every year at our annual July 4 neighborhood picnic. It wasn't based on winning a cash prize though. We both really loved my mother's fried chicken and the drumsticks were our favorites. Even combined, we never ate close to seventy-five drumsticks though, but only because my mom didn't fry that many chickens.

And I never won either. My brother had the appetite of a hockey team and he was a much faster eater than I was so he always got more drumsticks. That still sticks in my craw.

I told you I'd get to chickens.

How to Plan a Family Reunion—or Get Out of Planning One

WHEN I WAS A CHILD I daydreamed of living alone in a chicken coop in our backyard. Not the one with the chickens in it. No, my chicken coop would be decked out—and clean. My parents would bring me food and none of my nine brothers and sisters would ever enter unless I invited them. I'd feel guilty admitting this publicly if I didn't know some of them used to wish I lived in the chicken coop too.

Anyway, I'll bet they had similar fantasies, though theirs may have featured better accommodations. You like your space when you grow up with nine siblings in a three-bedroom house with only one bathroom.

Things have changed. We've gone our separate ways. We all have plenty of bathrooms. But we still crave our space. That's why for our annual sibling reunion we take over a church camp. My family has me plan the event, maybe because I'm the most organized one in the bunch. Or because I live closest. Or because I can't say no.

Whatever the reason, it's up to me. When you throw in spouses and some of the kids and grandkids, our family gatherings are a little like a zoo with the lions loose—a lot of running around and screaming going on.

But after years of planning the event I consider myself an expert. I don't know how your reunion will turn out if you use the tips below but I do know you'll be asked to organize it again next time. At least it works for me.

1. Schedule carefully for maximum attendance and convenience. You already know you should avoid having a reunion when school is in session. But did you know you should never, ever have a family reunion during an election year?

2. Keep in mind the reunion planner's mantra which, incidentally, is the same as the real estate agent's mantra: location, location, location. If some of your relatives won't come for the family, they may come for the local attractions.

3. Remember, one of the most crucial parts of any family gathering is the food. That's why I don't cook it. The staff at the church camp do that for us. Fortunately they also do the clean-up, which is helpful because my siblings and I have a long history of fighting over whose turn it is to do the dishes.

4. Be willing to forgive and hope that everyone else in the family is too. A family is like a pile of cockleburs. They stick together but they can poke each other a little bit too. Don't let that spoil your gathering.

5. Remember, a reunion is a perfect time for a family photo. But be prepared for everyone to complain while you line them up to take it. That includes all those family members who've been taking selfies all day. Be firm though, because the minute the photo is taken they'll all ask you to send it to them.

6. And most importantly, pick the right family. I'm joking! It's probably too late for that. But if you can't pick your family you can at least pick the reunion that suits them. Mine prefers to spend the weekend hiking and shooting the bull—and there's a lot of bull. If I forced them to wear matching T-shirts and do scavenger hunts all weekend they might pick a new organizer. Hey, wait....

Hey, Greeting
Card Company

DEAR GREETING CARD PERSON,

I'm about to have a milestone birthday. I won't say which one but I'll give you a hint: It's not my tenth.

I'm writing to suggest some changes to your birthday card line and I hope you can implement them before my big day on August 9. Before I get into that though, let me share a little background.

I remember my fortieth birthday as clearly as if it were yesterday. It wasn't, and not by a long shot, but I still remember waking up feeling like I was twenty-one and ending the day feeling like I was seventy-seven.

I knew it would be that way. That's why I liked thirty-nine so much. It was the oldest I could be and still not be forty. I might've been thirty-nine years and 374 and a half days old but I was still not forty. Still, thirty-nine wasn't perfect either, mainly because no one ever believed me when I said that's what I was. Then I turned forty and learned what real abuse is.

It actually started the night before my birthday when I told my then four-year-old son I would be forty years old the next day. He asked innocently, "Are you going to be as old as Grandma?" Grandma was eighty-four at the time.

The next day a now former friend asked which birthday I was celebrating. When I told her she said, "I thought you were getting up there."

Up there? Forty isn't old. It used to be. But it isn't anymore, though it was without a doubt the oldest I'd been up to that point. It's also true that I thought it would take a lot longer to get there.

Then there were the cards. That's where you come in, Greeting Card Person. When I was young my birthday cards came with money and good wishes. Later they contained only wishes and not all of them good.

But starting on my fortieth birthday things really went downhill, and not just my cards. But let's stick with those. Ever since I turned forty my birthday cards have mainly contained insults and ridicule. You know, like "So many candles, so little breath." "You're not getting older. You're getting fatter." Very funny.

Even the well-wishes are thinly disguised insults. "Here's wishing you success in all you do. But you better get started. You're running out of time." Those kinds of wishes would make a fifth grader feel old.

This, Greeting Card Person, is why people don't discuss their age. Best to keep it to ourselves. Otherwise, if we don't feel old before our birthday, we will after it's over.

As I face another milestone I'm appealing to your

decency. Mature people deserve respect. So do I. And I know you can do better. Anyone can come up with insults, even me. And I'm not a professional greeting card person—or elected official or late-night talk show host. How about these:

Don't let anyone tell you you're old. Older people are wise and mature. And you're neither of those.

Welcome to middle age, that magical time in life when you see better in bright light but look better in dim.

Middle age is a great time to get tattoos; you have more room for them.

Don't let the fact that you were born in another century make you feel old. By the way, which century was that?

See? Easy. Also a lot more fun than it should be. But anyone can do that. You're experts. Why not put your skills to work creating cards that are respectful without being gooey? May I suggest something along these lines?

You deserve to be treated like a queen on your birthday. You relax while I clean your house and make dinner for you.

Happy birthday to one of the wisest people I know. You were right all along.

I'm so sorry for all the insulting birthday cards I've sent you over the years. They were the only ones on the rack.

The first two might be a stretch but the last one is almost true. So dear Greeting Card Person, I suggest you create a new line of birthday cards that honor the wisdom and knowledge those celebrating birthdays have gained. And if we haven't gained any, I don't think our special day is the best time to say so.

Winning the Birthday Party Competition

IF YOU ASK ME, children's birthday parties have gotten out of hand. I don't even recall having a birthday party when I was a child, let alone renting a swimming pool for one. But then we didn't have a swimming pool to rent in my hometown. We had a lake. And you didn't have to rent it but you did have to chase the cows off the beach.

Also my mother was busy. There were ten children in my family. One does not plan ten birthday parties a year unless one is a professional party planner.

Needless to say, I did attend birthday parties as a child. And I was once hurt deeply when, as I handed my gift to the birthday girl, she said with feeling, "I hope it's not another paint-by-number." I grew up in a very small town. The local hardware and drug stores had the only toy departments in town and I happen to know they both had fine selections of paint-by-number sets.

I was invited to a few other parties as a child but far fewer than my son attended when he was growing up—maybe because I had a reputation for giving paint-by-number sets. He went to parties at arcades, hotels and fast food restaurants. He attended swimming parties, skating parties, paintball parties and even a disco party. As a result, he always hoped his mother would come up with something equally as exciting. Poor thing, he had the wrong mother.

My birthday party-deprived childhood left me completely unprepared to plan birthday parties that could compete with the modern variety. I never even made what you could call a real birthday cake. That's what bakeries are for. I did put five candles in the peanut butter sandwich I made for my son's fifth birthday breakfast. He loved peanut butter sandwiches, so I never made waffles either.

It didn't mean I loved him less. Here's what I told people who made their children cakes in the shape of cartoon characters or choo-choo trains: "After work every day I have just a few hours to spend with my son. I could spend that time making a birthday cake in the shape of a train, or I could get down on my hands and knees and actually play train with him. I choose the latter." I don't mention that I couldn't make a train cake if I tried.

Unfortunately, homemade theme cakes and matching party paraphernalia were and probably still are an important part of birthday parties for the elementary school set. While I distributed store-bought birthday cake at one of my lackluster parties, a young guest told me that his mother actually made his birthday cakes. I told him I love my son too much to do that to him.

The child persisted. "Usually," he said, "homemade tastes better." I said, "That depends on whose home it was made in. Now eat your cake or I will."

Along with my lack of experience, birthday party horror stories added to my anxiety. At a birthday party thrown by some friends, a blindfolded guest missed the piñata and whacked another partygoer. A friend's daughter broke her arm at a birthday party. And a little boy brought unwanted guests to one of my nephew's parties: head lice.

Another issue for me was the gifts. Ten guests meant ten gifts and while I know he would have disagreed, I thought my child needed more toys like I need more dirty dishes in my sink.

And then there was that small matter of being responsible for other people's children when I wasn't sure I was even qualified to care for my own.

But above all I was intimidated by stories of sensational children's parties where the parents rented a limousine, hired a celebrity entertainer or took all the guests to Disneyland. My idea of a good party is one where there's plenty of guacamole, which many children don't seem to appreciate.

How could I compete? I couldn't. Nevertheless, I managed some semblance of a birthday party every year from the time my son was old enough to care until the time he no longer wanted me around for his birthday parties. Here's how I did it:

The Fast-Food Restaurant Option:

On the advice of a friend I called a fast-food restaurant to plan my son's fifth birthday party. I was happy to learn that the restaurant would supply not only kids' meals but a birthday cake as well. Their play area would provide the entertainment for the kids. That left me responsible only for sending invitations and picking out the birthday gift—or using the toy in the kid's meal, which I'm ashamed to admit I actually considered.

It sounded easy enough, but it was exhausting. Being in charge of eight five-year-olds is like supervising a roomful of grasshoppers. Still, it was a success by my criteria: No body parts were broken. Nobody wanted his gift back. Nobody wanted his mother before the party was over. At least no one mentioned it if he did, and this particular demographic group is not known for keeping their thoughts to themselves.

Even the birthday cake was a hit. It may not have looked like a choo-choo train or a cartoon character but it was decorated magnificently with the logo of a certain popular fast-food restaurant.

The Rent-An-Activity Option:

Another year I booked the party at a bowling alley. I did have some concerns—many small feet and many large bowling balls in the same room, to name one. But what could be more fun for a group of first graders than dropping large balls onto a shiny, hardwood floor?

This party might have been a success except for one thing. Four parents who had not bothered to RSVP brought their kids anyway—and then left. Suddenly we had nine children, but only one bowling lane. This did allow the kids plenty of time for activities between bowling. Unfortunately, we hadn't planned any.

The Sleepover Option:

A sleepover is one of the least expensive children's birthday parties you can have—unless you count pain and suffering. And it was one of my son's favorites. I didn't share his enthusiasm. For reasons I don't recall from my own childhood, when you're young it's a luxury to stay up late and feel miserable the next day.

Everyone knows a sleepover is not a sleepover. It could more accurately be called a layover, a brief layover. The only ones sleeping during a sleepover are the parents of the guests—not that they don't deserve it.

Even knowing the truth, many parents, beaten down by their child's pleading, consent to sleepovers. I learned a lot from the many sleepovers we had while my son was growing up, though I never learned to say no to them. Here are a few tips that should help you if you're still engaging in the birthday party competition.

First of all, keep it small. At one sleepover my son had four boys stay the night. This is a good number. Still, for some reason it seemed like a lot more.

Remain calm. It can be upsetting to have a child who is not your own run into your house screaming "I am bleeding to death!" Naturally it's upsetting to hear your own child scream that too, but you're better able to interpret his or her cries for the theatrics they are.

Use the television for the purpose for which it was intended: sedation. I'm not generally a fan of television, however a child's sleepover party is one time when it can be useful. Television is the opiate of the elementary school masses and it is a legal opiate. Use it.

Don't bother picking up until your guests have all gone

home. Certainly ask the children to clean up after themselves but do it from your place on the couch. Picking up with a house full of children is like shoveling snow during a blizzard or drying off while you're still in the shower.

Play games at bedtime, but not board games. Play head games. Tell the children that certainly they may wake up as early as they wish, but if they're the first to wake up they must lie perfectly still with their eyes closed until everyone else is awake. Hopefully it will be at least 6 a.m. before they begin to wonder how they'll know that everyone else is awake if they're lying perfectly still with their eyes closed.

Remember that unlike other parties, a sleepover is not over when the guests go home. Plan on devoting a great deal of time and energy to putting your home back in order. Be prepared to spend the next few weeks returning miscellaneous items such as toys, sleeping bags, jackets and dirty socks. Expect the birthday person to be cranky, disagreeable and not the least bit appreciative in the days following the birthday party. And finally, count on them to ask for another one next year.

Blame the AARP

IT'S A TRAUMATIC EVENT IN ANYONE'S LIFE. You're coasting along, going about your business, and one day you open your mailbox and there's a letter from the American Association of Retired Persons—AARP. Many a midlife crisis has been launched by birthday greetings from the AARP.

I remember when it happened to me. I was turning fifty in a month whether I wanted to or not, and somehow they knew. Truly, until I got the letter I'd been doing just fine with the milestone birthday. Oh, they were nice about it. For just $16 they offered me membership in their fine organization, a subscription to their award-winning magazine, discounts on a variety of services and my very own lobbyists in Washington. They don't call them lobbyists; they call them spokespeople. But I didn't just come out of the voting booth yesterday. I know that a spokesperson is nothing but a lobbyist working on my behalf instead of someone else's. This not only shows how gullible they think the electorate is, it shows how cynical I'm getting in my old age.

Anyway, there was more. If I signed up right away I'd get a free tote bag announcing to everyone everywhere that I'm a proud member of the AARP. I was thinking it would also announce that I'm over fifty—or that I stole someone's tote bag. And frankly I'm still not sure which of those I prefer to have everyone think.

I guess I was having a hard time picturing myself with an AARP card too. I like discounts as much as the next person. I've always wanted my own personal lobbyist/ spokesperson. And I'm not ashamed of my age. I certainly never saw much sense in lying about it. I don't want anyone thinking, "Wow, she looks rough for twenty-nine."

Anyway, fifty isn't old. It used to be but it isn't any more—especially now that I'm older than that. Fifty is the new thirty after all; and you never see thirty-year-olds carrying AARP tote bags.

Nevertheless, my letter from the AARP isn't the only evidence I have of my advancing age. For one thing, I'm increasingly opinionated—but only because I'm always right. Some would say I'm set in my ways but what can I do? My ways are the best ways. And I may have become some- what cantankerous. Oh, wait. I've always been that way.

I admit I check the obituaries more often than I used to. And I find the older I get the more I'm annoyed by that old Billy Joel song, "Only the Good Die Young." It's offensive and not much of an incentive to improve.

I occasionally find fault with the younger generation— much like the previous generation finds fault with mine, and the one before that found fault with them and so on right back to Eve who once told Adam that finding fault with the next generation is the first sign of aging. That was after he'd criticized Cain and Abel, but the way they behaved, who could blame him for that?

I've started wearing more comfortable clothing, though that isn't necessarily a sign of getting older. I think it's a sign of getting wiser.

And I find myself daydreaming about buying a sports car and getting a tattoo. I'm joking. But seriously if I'm in the throes of a full-blown midlife crisis it wasn't brought on by my age. I blame the AARP.

Born to Be Tame

THERE'S A ROAR IN THE AIR. There's no place to park. There are waiting lines at every restaurant in town and higher prices at all the gas stations and hotels. There's one big round-the-clock party going on. It can only mean one thing: my birthday!

Well, that and the extra five hundred thousand or so people in town for the annual Sturgis Motorcycle Rally and Races. Each year bikers from all over the world descend upon the Black Hills of South Dakota for the "granddaddy of all bike gatherings," as it's promoted. (I know it's sexist but calling it the "grandmother" of all bike gatherings might get you killed.)

Some of those five hundred thousand probably pass right through your town on their way here. If it's early August and they're roaring by on two wheels, they're probably on their way to the rally. And because Sturgis is normally just the right size for the seven thousand or so people who live there the rest of the year, some of these visitors naturally spill over into nearby towns, including mine, Rapid City, which is about half an hour away.

Throughout the weeklong event, which is stretched to several weeks by visitors who arrive early and stay late, there are two songs running through my head. The first is "Happy Birthday" since my birthday is August 9. (Make a note of it.)

The second is "Born to Be Wild." Not that that describes me. There's just something about the roar of a couple hundred thousand motorcycles that inspires one to sing it right out loud—whether or not one can sing.

I don't like to admit this but "Born to Be Bland" might be more like it. Born to ride in air-conditioned comfort. Born to be in bed by ten and up by five. I might be better suited to the "grandmother" of all bike gatherings.

"Wild" for me would be having my ears pierced a second time. Driving five miles over the speed limit. Putting sugar in my iced tea.

During most of the year I'm wallpaper. But during the rally I'm unique or, at the very least, peculiar. When I attend the rally, which I have a few times, I stand out among the five hundred thousand rugged individualists there. I'm the one with no tattoos. I'm the one who arrived by car. I'm the one wearing all of my clothing—and none of it black leather. I'm not sure but I don't think my wallet is even real leather. (They don't use Velcro on leather goods, do they?)

While I'm bemoaning my dullness, my husband is making noises about getting a motorcycle. This seems very selfish to me since I'm the one with the birthday.

But, actually he makes those noises all year long; they're just louder during the rally. They have to be, to be heard above the roar. To hear him talk the only thing standing between him and a Harley is me. I gently remind him that there is also that little matter of many thousands of dollars, which is a much more formidable obstacle than I'll ever be, believe it or not.

He tells me he already has a motorcycle license. I tell him the first time I rode on a motorcycle the driver nearly wrecked it. He had a license too.

He tells me I could see the country from the back of a bike. I tell him what I love about traveling with him is reading and napping while he drives. Neither seems prudent on a motorcycle.

He tells me that when you ride a motorcycle you're so much closer to the natural world. I tell him yes, the wind is in your hair and the bugs are in your teeth.

He tells me he's always, always wanted a Harley, and if he had one he'd never want another thing...except for maybe a Triumph TR6...and a PT Cruiser...and....

I tell him that's great. But I'm the one with the birthday. Shouldn't we be talking about what I want? "You're right," he admits sheepishly. "How would you feel about a Harley 1200 Sportster?"

A Bad Case of CRS

MY FRIEND "SUSAN" TELLS ME she wants to get a make-over and lose twenty pounds—by Friday. It's Wednesday.

"Do you, by chance, have a certain milestone event coming up?" I asked her. She nods glumly. I knew it. Susan is exhibiting the classic symptoms of CRS—Class Reunion Syndrome. The moment anyone decides to attend their reunion, they're overcome with the urge to diet, exercise and maybe even have a little "work" done.

I never went that far, but I once had some work *undone* for a reunion. I was worried I'd be the first person in history to wear braces to a fortieth class reunion. The only thing worse would be wearing dentures to a twentieth. But thank-fully I got my braces off in the nick of time and I didn't even have to threaten the orthodontist.

But I would have. There's just something about a class reunion that makes you desperate. Maybe it's the memories of bullies, wedgies and D minuses. Maybe it's the fear of being called your old high school nickname.

Whatever it is, as the date of the reunion gets closer those with CRS may start having second thoughts. They may even attempt to come up with good, though not necessarily honest, reasons why they can't attend after all. "It's so hard to get a pet sitter." "I might have a kidney stone by then." "The weather is so unpredictable in August."

In the days before the reunion CRS victims may find themselves digging through old year books and stalking former classmates on social media. This is partly out of genuine curiosity. But it's also an effort to avoid that embarrassing moment when a classmate hugs them and says enthusiastically, "It's so nice to see you," and they have no idea who it is.

I don't mean to brag but I can name every single person I graduated with. It helps that there were only twenty-eight of us. I admit though, that at a reunion several years ago I didn't recognize a woman I once knew very well. In my defense let me say it was a multiclass reunion and she was from another class. Also she had really aged.

That leads me to another common CRS symptom: The satisfying, though usually mistaken, sense that everyone looks older—except you.

CRS sufferers may also notice that when they open their mouths during the reunion stories fall out. Some of them may even be true. But a fair number would be better left untold. At one of my high school reunions a classmate was telling the tale of a joyride in a "borrowed" police car when someone interrupted him to ask, "Aren't you running for county commissioner?"

Towards the end of the evening those suffering from CRS may find themselves saying, "Let's stay in touch," or "Call me when you're in town." That's because by this time CRS has generally run its course, though those who've experienced it are apt to relapse in five or ten years.

Maturing

THE NEWSPAPER ARTICLE SAID a hostile ex-husband had sent his class reunion committee an "edited" version of his ex-wife's biography. I don't recall all the details, but he apparently listed drug addiction and grand larceny among her many achievements. He claimed jail was her current residence. I believe the article also mentioned a pending libel suit.

There is something about a class reunion that brings out the desperation in all of us—even if it's only our five-year high school reunion. (Not that it is.) Demographers could refer to the years leading up to the early reunions in our life as the RNDs, or RAMEN NOODLE DAYS. Those living in the RNDs are trying on careers, paying off college loans and buying cars they can't afford. As they approach their first class reunion reunionites hope to marry quickly so they can show off a trophy spouse to former classmates. And they'd like to get a really nice tan and lose ten pounds.

Once at the reunion newlyweds cling to each other, drink out of the same glass and eat off the same hors d'oeuvres plate—behavior they will find nauseating in five years. At these early reunions there is much boisterous talk of the outlandish shenanigans from school days. Reunionites may have improved slightly with age—their stories, unfortunately, have not.

Demographers might refer to those individuals approaching their next few reunions as BWD or BURDENED WITH DEBT. BWDs have taken on mortgages and set up college funds for their children. They've worked hard to establish themselves in careers and they can't wait to tell their former classmates that they've published a novel or taken over a corporation—even if they haven't.

And before the reunion BWDs would like to get a really nice tan and lose fifteen pounds too. Like the rest of us they'd love to be as thin as they were back when they first started thinking they were fat.

By this time most reunionites have very nice partners but they no longer consider them trophies. Once at the reunion they leave them in the corner with the other spouses and huddle with former classmates to brag about the children.

By the time the next reunion rolls around the marriage is over and the children are in college—or jail, which is cheaper. This phase in life could be called HOUSE EMPTY/ LOTS OF LIABILITES or HELL. Reunionites are still telling the same stories but with less enthusiasm. Tales of your own youthful mischief aren't nearly as funny after you've bailed your progeny out of jail.

Prior to the reunion reunionites hope to lose twenty pounds. They've also started avoiding the sun and all those wrinkle causing rays. Demographers might call reunionites looking forward to the latter get-togethers in life as GOM or GRANDPARENTS ON THE MOVE. If their income has not caught up with their outgo, at least their outgo is going out more slowly. The kids have finished college, the house is paid for and the reunion is just a stop on the road to the next RV park.

Feeling less responsible for their children now that they're grown, GOMs are back to rehashing the mischief of their youth—and condemning the behavior of the younger generation.

GOMs have ceased to be concerned about their weight or the condition of their skin. A lifetime has taught them that vanity is a waste of time and there are far more important ways to spend their energy. Plus they feel darn lucky just to be alive.

Celebrating Work
Easier than Doing It

LABOR DAY IS ALWAYS CELEBRATED the first Monday in September. That's because, even back in the 1800s when Congress made it a federal holiday, everyone wanted to sleep in on Monday mornings.

After you finally wake up this Labor Day I invite to join me in thinking about work. Don't do any. Just think about it. Think about the jobs you've had and all they've taught you. Think about how what you've done for a living has formed you into the unique person you are. After that think about going back to bed. You've earned the rest.

I spent the majority of my working life as a public relations professional for a wonderful nonprofit. But like many people my first jobs were in the restaurant business, first as a dishwasher and then as a server. There are few better jobs for teaching one about human behavior than waiting tables. People are cranky when they're tired and hungry.

And they get crankier when you forget to put their order in or bring them a chicken dinner when they ordered a ribeye.

But as a teenager the hardest part for me was that people got hungry so darned early in the morning. And when you wait tables the size of your income depends entirely on how friendly, efficient and awake you are all day, every day. I happen to know that when you're tired yourself, it's hard to be friendly to people who haven't had their coffee yet.

I also learned about faith and forgiveness working at a restaurant. Every Sunday morning the church crowd rushed in, everyone hoping to enjoy one of the restaurant's famous caramel rolls. I don't recall the exact order now, but let's say the Lutherans dismissed first. That left the Congregationalists praying, "Oh Lord, let there be caramel rolls left." Often there were not, partly because the Catholics usually had services on Saturday night and the agnostics had no schedule at all. Watching the ensuing chaos, I learned how hard it is to practice brotherly love and forgiveness when one sits through a church service dreaming of caramel rolls and gets beat out by another denomination.

After I left the restaurant I worked for a short stint at a drive-in where I learned that when you get to eat your mistakes, you tend to make more of them.

I was working at a hardware store the day Elvis died. Other days too. I just remember that day more clearly than the rest. I do know the majority of my time was spent dusting which was lucky because I knew nothing about hardware. I'm proud to say that by the time I left for college I'd learned a few things; for example, a ten-penny nail doesn't cost ten pennies and it's a "joist," not a "joyce."

My only other retail job was in a state park gift shop where I worked one summer while I was in college. The main lesson one learns in retail is that when someone says, "The customer is always right," what they really mean is, "The customer is the one with the money and if we want it, we need to treat him as though he's always right whether he is or not."

The following summer I cleaned cabins in Yellowstone National Park and I learned to appreciate people who do the job for longer than three months. Cleaning up after other people is hard work. It requires attention to detail and commitment to quality and no one even notices unless you do it badly. Plus when you're a housekeeper there are all those beds and you can't even nap.

It was also while I was in college that I began my career in radio, first as a news person. My boss called me after one of my first newscasts to tell me that before my next one I'd better change my name to Ann. He didn't think anyone would take me seriously as Dorothy (and your little dog too!). I'm not sure anyone took me seriously as Ann either, especially changing my name mid-shift like that.

Eventually I became an announcer so it no longer mattered if anyone took me seriously. I spent the next ten years playing requests, giving the weather and sitting through countless sports broadcasts. While living in a small town in Iowa I worked for a daytime station which broadcast every sporting event the local students participated in. The broadcasts were carried over phone lines exactly like regular calls except that when a game was coming in the receiver was still in its cradle and the buttons on the phone didn't light up. Even a thinking person could forget the phone was in use. And I wasn't always thinking.

One night after two back-to-back basketball games, I signed off the station late and went home, only to be awakened by the phone at 5:30 a.m. My boss had discovered that I'd never disconnected the phone line. The station had been making a long-distance phone call for...oh...about fifteen hours. Fortunately I didn't lose my job, but I'm still paying off the phone bill. Thank goodness for weekend rates.

In my current profession as a writer I've come to see the value in all of my work experiences, both the good and the bad. To misuse an old saying, that which doesn't kill you gives you something else to write about.

A Bad Case of Friggatriskaidekaphobia

MORE THAN SEVENTEEN MILLION AMERICANS suffer from friggatriskaidekaphobia, also known as paraskevidekatria-phobia, though they seldom admit it, mainly because they can't pronounce it.

Loosely translated, paraskevidekatriaphobia means, "I'd like to buy a vowel, Pat." I'm joking. Actually it's a fear of Friday the 13th. And friggatriskaidekaphobia comes from two words: Frigga, the Norse goddess for whom Friday is named, and triskaidekaphobia, which is an irrational fear of large words.

Kidding again! Triskaidekaphobia is a fear of the number thirteen. But there is a word for the fear of large words. It's hippopotomonstrosesquipedaliophobia and I didn't just make that up. I don't have that much time.

If it weren't for the cut and paste function on my computer I'd be writing about Candy Corn Day which is

October 30th instead. But this is an important and timely topic since we have a Friday the 13th coming up on, well, the next Friday the 13th. We get one every time the month begins on Sunday and that can happen up to three times a year. So I think it's high time we get our paraskevidekatriaphobia under control.

If you're going to be afraid of a day it makes sense it would be Friday the 13th. Tuesday the 12th and Saturday the 5th just doesn't have the historical baggage.

Friday's bad rap may have its roots in Christian tradition. Jesus was crucified on a Friday, and some people think Eve gave Adam the apple on a Friday and that Cain killed Abel on a Friday. That seems like pure speculation to me though since the calendar hadn't been invented yet.

Poor number thirteen has always had a bad reputation too, and through no fault of its own. Traditionally twelve is like a favorite child, perfect in every way. There are twelve months in a year, twelve signs of the zodiac and twelve days of Christmas. Somehow that makes thirteen less than perfect and even unlucky. By that logic fourteen on up should be downright dangerous. And why does eleven get off so easy?

Nevertheless, the result is high rises without thirteenth floors, airports without thirteenth gates and airplanes without thirteenth aisles. I don't mean to worry anyone but I think the thirteenth floor is the thirteenth floor whether you call it the fourteenth or fifty-fifth. Calling it anything else makes a fool out of us and a liar out of the guy who puts the numbers on the elevator buttons.

There's even an old superstition that says if you have thirteen letters in your name you're cursed. Believers in this theory point out that many notorious murderers had names with thirteen letters in them. I would point out that many other notorious murderers didn't. But there are Charles Manson, Jeffrey Dahmer, Theodore Bundy and Jack the Ripper. But I doubt very much that Jack's surname was "the Ripper," and if it was it's no wonder he turned out like he did.

Anyway, before I was married I also had thirteen letters in my name and I somehow managed to refrain from becoming a serial killer. I now have twelve letters and I'm as perfect as a dozen eggs just like Elvis Presley, Oprah Winfrey and Mother Teresa. Oh wait. Mother Teresa was born Anjezë Gonxhe Bojaxhiu, in case you ever get that question in Trivial Pursuit.

If you ask me the friggatriskaidekaphobia issue was made worse in 1980 with the release of the horror movie, *Friday the* 13th. That's when the world was introduced to a hockey mask-wearing killer named Jason. I never saw the movie because I was afraid it would ruin Friday the 13th for me in the same way the movie *Psycho* ruined showers for me. Don't worry, I still take them.

Whatever the reason, the fear of Friday the 13th has serious consequences. Millions of Americans suffer unnecessary anxiety and businesses suffer millions of dollars in lost revenue because so many people call in sick with a bad case of friggatriskaidekaphobia.

If you're living in a friggatriskaidekaphobic prison of your own making, you could stay home on Friday the 13th, wrap yourself in bubble wrap, and play Scrabble using the new words you've just learned.

Or like me you could go about your business, confident that you'll be as safe as you are any other day and maybe safer. With all the friggatriskaidekaphobes staying home there should be fewer people on the road.

I'd go so far as to say Friday the 13th is a lucky day. Most students would tell you any Friday is a lucky Friday. Most teachers too.

And if it's the thirteen that's bothering you consider the term "baker's dozen." You eat the extra doughnut in the car on the way home and the family doesn't even suspect because they sent you out for a dozen. Lucky you.

A Haunting Dilemma

HALLOWEEN ISN'T MY FAVORITE HOLIDAY, partly because it doesn't involve a day off. There are really only two things I like about it: candy and small children wearing costumes, neither of which you really need Halloween for.

But whether I like it or not, here we are. 'Tis the season when normally sane people put on creepy costumes, buy wheelbarrows full of candy for the neighborhood children and go off to haunted houses. Not me. I dress as an eccentric middle-aged woman on Halloween, same as I do every other holiday.

I do load up on Halloween candy but it's not for the kids. We don't get that many trick-or-treaters where I live. Maybe my costume scares them away.

And I'll never go to another haunted house, even if they leave the lights on for me. Halloween is already plenty scary for me. I don't think it's a coincidence that Halloween comes just before the scariest day of the year: Election Day. I don't need skeletons popping out of the dark to startle me. I jump when someone honks at me at a stoplight, especially if I've dozed off.

I have a traumatic memory of seeing the movie *Jaws* many years ago. If you've ever seen it you remember the dreadful music that warned everyone except the actors that the shark was coming. If only they'd been able to hear that music they might have survived to see the credits.

At one point while the scary music was playing, my younger brother snuck up behind me and goosed me. I screamed and jumped four feet out of my seat. The audience laughed like they were at a showing of *Dumb and Dumber* instead of *Jaws*.

Yes, some people might say I'm jumpy but I prefer to say I have well-developed reflexes. People who can go through haunted houses (or watch *Jaws*) and not jump out of their socks obviously have sluggish reflexes and probably shouldn't be allowed to operate motorized vehicles.

I don't need blood-curdling screams or zombies coming at me to scare me either. I'm terrified when a spider crawls out of my cupboard. Or when my grocery store moves everything around. Or when a computer person tells me it's time to update my software.

My to-do list scares me. So does an extra-long line at a public restroom. I saw a "beware of the dog" sign on an open gate this morning and my heart rate still hasn't come down.

I live in fear of someone offering to show me all their vacation photos. Or that I'll run out of Halloween candy and have to start handing out canned vegetables.

And I don't need fake blood and goblin goo to gross me out. I'm disgusted when I see a ball player spit. Or when I have to dig gum off the bottom of my shoe. Or when I find a hair in my food, even if it's mine. And I'm practically nauseated by what I find in my kitchen sink drain basket after I do dishes, which is why I put off doing dishes so long.

I bet you're thinking I'm scared of everything. Am not! I'm not afraid of flying. I read that more than twenty million Americans are, but I'm not and here's why: A lot of people go on trips and most of them come back.

Some people are afraid of cemeteries. Not me. I lived next to one for years and I never had a problem with my neighbors.

And some people are afraid to go to a dentist. I'm not—unless the dentist has cavities.

I've heard people fear public speaking more than death. But if you give me the choice to speak or die, you won't be able to shut me up.

People are scared of all sorts of things: germs, birds, clowns, doctors. None of those bother me in the least—unless you put them in a haunted house.

Knowing how I feel about them, you may be surprised to learn that I've not only been to haunted houses, but it was also once my job to persuade other unsuspecting souls to attend them. For many years I was the public relations person for a non-profit that hosted an annual free haunted house for the public. A vegetarian probably wouldn't make the best spokesperson for cattle producers. A Prius owner might have a hard time selling Humvees. And chickens probably shouldn't promote haunted houses. I don't mean actual chickens. They can promote whatever they want. I mean fraidy-cat chickens like me.

But that's exactly what I did. Then all the while I was telling people how terrific our haunted house was, I was thinking, "There's no such thing as a terrific haunted house." In the public relations business, this is called "lying."

But I was being completely honest when I told them that I'd once gone to the haunted house and it scared me so badly that I'd never been back.

I'd actually gone twice, but one of those times they'd left the lights on, so I'm not sure that counts. It was the morning after the haunted house and I had to walk across the street to the building where it was, by then, being dismantled. Along the way I met up with a friend who hadn't heard about the haunted house. I realize that doesn't speak well for my skills as a promoter.

I asked her to walk along so we could talk, but I was unaware that she was unaware, so I failed to warn her about what we might see when we entered the building. And what we saw was lots and lots of blood. She didn't stick around long enough to find out it was fake.

I'm proud to say that unlike my now former friend, I was unfazed by the haunted house in broad daylight. It wasn't my blood we were looking at.

The other time I attended the haunted house it was actually the morning before it opened, and the lights were off. A handful of employees were invited to "test" it. I worked for a company made up of compassionate people who served others. It was daytime and it was the organizer's first attempt at a haunted house. How bad could it be? I'll tell you. It was torture. I hated it. I thought it would never end, which is, I suppose, a resounding endorsement of a haunted house.

The Great Candy Exchange

IT WAS A LONG TIME AGO but I still remember the first time I took my son trick-or-treating. I stood beside him as he carefully chose treats from the heaping bowls held by our neighbors. I had to bite my tongue to keep from whispering, "No! Not that one! I don't like SweeTARTS! I mean, *you* don't like SweeTARTS." Then in between stops, I coached him, "Remember, when given a choice, always choose chocolate. Now go get 'em Batman!"

We came home early from that first outing and I put him to bed after two small pieces of candy. He was young; he needed his sleep. Then, being a responsible parent some of the time, I carefully looked through his loot for safety reasons. Plus I was dying to know what he got. It wasn't bad for a rookie.

Naturally there was a lot of candy he didn't care for— or maybe I didn't care for it. But there was also plenty of the good stuff—and by good stuff I mean chocolate. In my opinion if it isn't chocolate, it's a waste of fat and sugar. You may feel differently. Back then, if you were one of those people who snitched the hard candy, licorice and Bit-O-Honeys your children brought home on Halloween night, I would have happily traded you for all their chocolate. In fact, that's kind of what I did.

After checking out my son's take for the night, I had a brilliant idea. I unloaded a bunch of his non-chocolate treats on the older trick-or-treaters that came by our house later. That saved him a lot of artificial coloring, preservatives and goo in his teeth. And it saved for me more of the chocolate bars I bought to give away. That became my Halloween tradition, at least until my son was old enough to start wondering what happened to all his Jolly Ranchers and Laffy Taffy.

Don't act so shocked. You know as well as I do that Halloween is just an excuse for adults to stock up on their favorites. Then they give their treats to other people's children and other parents give treats to their children. And were it not for the net increase created by empty nesters doling out goodies, everyone could just as well keep their kids home on Halloween and feed them their own candy for supper.

Instead they send their children out into the cold dark night, hoping they'll be safe, have fun and bring home treats they enjoy at least as much as what they bought to give away. It's the Great Candy Exchange.

Now that I'm an empty nester myself, my son is no longer around to gather up undesirable candy for me to give away. And I'm sure not going to buy anything I don't like. There could be leftovers. And there probably will be.

To be on the safe side I buy enough Halloween candy for about a hundred trick-or-treaters. Our average is ten. But you never know.

There are people who have so many trick-or-treaters they spend all of Halloween evening sitting on their front step passing out goodies like they're on a jellybean assembly line. Eventually they run out of candy and finish the night off hoping they won't be tricked for giving away Ramen Noodles and instant oatmeal.

But I live at the top of a big hill that isn't well lit. If they only knew, kids all over town would flock to my neighborhood with their flashlights and hike up the hill to my house. Every year I buy enough chocolate treats that I could give a heaping handful to every trick-or-treater who comes to my door. I don't, but I could.

Out of Costume

AMONG MY MANY FAILINGS AS A MOTHER, add to the list the fact that I never made my son a Halloween costume. I took him trick-or-treating; I checked his treats for dangerous tricks. And I kept him from overdoing it on candy by helping myself to his stash when he wasn't looking. But I never made a costume. I'm just not the crafty sort. I can sew on a button and stitch up a hem if I absolutely must. But the last thing I sewed with an actual sewing machine was my thumb, and that has a way of inspiring you to look for other hobbies.

It doesn't help that I've never enjoyed wearing costumes myself. When I was growing up my Halloween costumes consisted mostly of those hard plastic masks that stayed on my face only because the elastic string got tangled in my hair.

I dressed up as Charlie Chaplin at some point in my adulthood but generally I have steadfastly avoided costume parties. I once found myself in the midst of a crowd of people headed to one while I was visiting a gambling town. It was late October and my husband and I rode the shuttle from our hotel to the casinos downtown. We soon discovered that we were the only ones not on the way to a costume party. We looked painfully out of place, though we told everyone we met that we were a young, hip duo dressed as an over-the-hill married couple. It still bothers me that so many people believed us.

On the shuttle with us were a dozen or so witches, five or six Draculas, a few cowboys, one cowgirl, one Superman and several loose-looking women. Most of the latter's costumes would never work for me. It's cold in late October and a lady of the evening wearing fleece and wool socks doesn't look right.

I have appeared in several theatre productions, but someone far more creative than I am always came up with my costumes. And I had some wardrobe malfunctions during my drama career that may have contributed to my costume phobia. There was the slip that slipped during one performance. I had to wiggle and squirm to keep it from landing around my ankles. That made it hard to focus on my lines, plus the audience probably thought I had fleas.

During another play my leading man was supposed to light the cigarette I held. Neither of us are smokers and we couldn't get the darn thing to light. I wound up "smoking" an unlit cigarette during an entire scene. Foolish as it looked, that is how I prefer my cigarettes.

You're probably thinking that this is a lengthy justification for why I never had the ambition to create a Halloween costume for my only child. But the fact that I never made any costumes doesn't mean he never wore any homemade costumes. He once dressed as Inspector Jacque Clouseau from the Pink Panther movies. The idea was his; the trench coat was mine, and he tramped around our entire neighborhood with it dragging on the ground—a safety no-no and a drycleaner's nightmare.

Fortunately you can buy costumes and I bought many of them, including several soldiers, Batman and a Star Wars storm trooper. And as far as I know, no one ever withheld candy from my son because he wasn't wearing a homemade costume. Nor did I ever ask any of the trick-or-treaters that came to my door if their costumes were homemade. But if a frumpy middle-aged couple ever shows up at my door asking for candy, I may have some questions.

Suffering for Suffrage

ELECTIONS BRING OUT THE WORST IN PEOPLE, just like thunderstorms bring out earthworms and manure piles bring out flies.

To save you some heartache, I'm going to gaze into my crystal ball and tell you exactly what's going to happen between now and the next election. That way you can take a vacation from social media and cable news until it's all over but the voting.

First we'll have the candidates, some of whom think that just because they're opinionated they should be in charge. There are also plenty who are motivated by power, greed or a chance to see themselves on a billboard. But most are running for office because they sincerely want to make the world better. And I, for one, am grateful that someone wants the job and is willing to run. I cannot imagine the courage and stamina it takes to survive the gauntlet that is a political campaign. I just watch and I can hardly stand it.

And the campaigns will be as brutal as ever. Candidates will have access to the most expensive free speech money can buy, and how will they use it? They'll recount every mistake their opponent has made dating back to fifth grade, call them dim-witted evildoers or worse and then challenge them to run a positive campaign focusing on the issues.

And at the end of every ad, they'll say, "I'm So-and-So and I approve of this message." And we'll think, "Really. You approve of that?" That right there ought to tell us something about them.

Then there's us, the electorate, though electorate is a funny name to call us when the only electing many of us do is electing not to take part. I know you vote though. And I do. And we both mind our manners too. But as we near the election, plenty of people we know will behave as badly as the party they think behaves badly.

Facebook users will rant and rave and share stories so bizarre they could only come from tabloid journalists, Russian fiction writers or the other candidate's campaign staff.

Some of their friends will like what they post and some will unfriend them. And some will threaten to move to Canada if the other side wins, much to the pleasure of the other side and the dismay of Canadians.

There will be polls and more polls. One side will point to them and say, "See. The American people love us." The other side will say, "We don't pay attention to polls." And when the polls switch so will their opinions about polls.

One side will tune into Cable News Channel A and the other side will tune into Cable News Channel B just to reassure themselves they're still right about everything.

The pundits will blather on. Those who agree with them will think they should be canonized. Those who don't will think they should be cannon fodder.

There will be news and there will be fake news and there will be much disagreement about which is which.

Watching all of this, you will be convinced that great waves of stupid are washing over this land. But take heart. Eventually Election Day will arrive, and not a moment too soon. If the campaign went on any longer we'd all spontaneously combust.

Some people will vote; many will not. And in the end someone will win. I'm sorry my crystal ball doesn't tell me who, and after you read all this way. But it does tell me that billions of dollars will have been spent, enough to repair every road and bridge in the country, bring every school up to par and pay every politician's legal bills.

The two sides will finally agree on one thing. They're happy it's over—for now.

And no one will move to Canada, much to the relief of the Canadians. They've seen how we act during election years.

I Frigi-dare You

HALLOWEEN IS NOT THE MOST TERRIFYING HOLIDAY of the year and not by a long shot. In fact, Halloween is actually a warmup act for the scariest holiday, National Clean Out Your Refrigerator Day, which is widely celebrated on November 15. Actually "widely" might be an exaggeration. "Celebrated" might be a stretch too.

National Clean Out Your Refrigerator Day was created in 1999 by home economists at Whirlpool Home Appliances to encourage us to empty our refrigerators of all the long-forgotten leftovers that will never be eaten in order to make room for all the Thanksgiving leftovers that will never be eaten.

I observed National Clean Out Your Refrigerator Day once and only once. Here's my story:

A few years ago, a guest in my home was attacked... by a ghost...in my refrigerator. She opened the door and it started throwing condiments at her. She ducked and let out a blood-curdling scream. Or maybe that was the milk curdling. Anyway, I can't blame her—or the milk. Our refrigerator is haunted.

My husband, who doesn't believe in ghosts, apologized to our startled guest and calmly picked up the ketchup, mustard and hot sauce bottles. As usual, he excused this bizarre event by pointing out that two of the shelves on the refrigerator door are busted and held in place with duct tape—more or less. I let my guest believe that. I didn't want the incident disturbing her sleep later. But I knew it was the ghost.

Our refrigerator is close to thirty years old, which is around 210 in refrigerator years. It's trauma and tragedy that lead to haunting, and a lot of both take place in the life of a household appliance in 210 years. Ours withstood a move across town. It stored countless cooking disasters. And scariest of all, it endured our teenager, his teenage friends and five teenage exchange students. That is no small thing. Many teens have a peculiar habit of opening and closing the refrigerator again and again like someone might have made a cheesecake in the last minute and a half. I can assure you, that in our home no one ever has.

It's a wonder our refrigerator is still humming along, though it hums a lot louder than it did when we bought it. Also, "humming" doesn't begin to describe the sounds emanating from our refrigerator. There are groans and sighs and occasional shrieks. I could swear I once heard the ghost say, "Feed me." Or maybe it said, "Clean me."

I'd like to say our refrigerator has lasted 210 years because we've taken such good care of it, but I hate to lie this early in an essay. We've failed at the little maintenance it requires—cleaning the coils on a regular basis. We don't have dust bunnies under there; we have dust bulldogs. And lately it's developed a wobble as though there are more bulldogs on one side.

We rarely clean it. It's too scary to go in there. That's why I like to eat out. The door squeaks on its hinges as you open it. Then you feel a...chill.

And it's dark. The lights haven't worked in years and replacing the bulbs doesn't help. We've tried. My naïve husband says there's a short somewhere. I say the ghost is at it again.

Food often goes missing in our dark refrigerator. Then I blame my husband for eating the last slice of pizza or chicken drumstick. I find it later while I'm crawling around in there with a flashlight looking for something else. My husband is vindicated, but I see no reason to mention it.

Despite being haunted, our fridge continues to carry out the most basic functions of a refrigerator: keeping drinking water cold and preserving leftovers for future generations. It doesn't seem right to replace such a reliable appliance just because it groans and shrieks and occasionally hurls a jar of mustard across the room. Nobody's perfect.

But then a few weeks ago another guest in our home had a run-in with the ghost. As they were unpacking for their stay with us, her husband foolishly placed a tiny bottle of her eye medicine in our haunted refrigerator—or *said* he did. She was unable to find it. And as the host, I felt compelled to look. I didn't see the medicine either. More extreme measures were called for.

I decided to face my fears, find the medicine and get a jump on National Clean Out Your Refrigerator Day. I put on my goggles, my gloves, my hard hat and my headlamp and I told my guests, "I'm going in. If I'm not back in three days call for help." And then, adrenaline coursing through my veins, I set off to boldly go where no one with any common sense has gone before. And what I found in the depths of my icebox was...chilling. Also, scary. Here's a sample:

- A bowl of shriveled brains. Or maybe it was month-old macaroni salad. It was one of those.
- A bag of swamp scum that may have been cilantro in another life.
- A handful of mummified grapes. I know what you're thinking: Those are called raisins. But I never buy raisins. These had definitely been grapes when we met.
- A concoction of every liquid that has ever been spilled in our fridge collected, congealed and coagulated in the bottom. It looked like there'd been a murder on a gumbo mud flat.
- Some creepy condiments, a menacing meat loaf and an assortment of other unidentifiable items, none of which were edible and from the looks of them, it was hard to believe they ever were. I was petrified just looking at them. So were they.

That's just some of what I found in the bowels of my haunted refrigerator. Here's what I didn't find: my guest's eye medicine. I suspect the ghost.

Useless Stuff Day

MARK YOUR CALENDAR! The official start of the holiday season is the third Thursday of November when we celebrate Use Less Stuff Day, not to be confused with Useless Stuff Day which for many of us falls on December 25.

The average American throws away almost five pounds of trash every day. Use Less Stuff Day is a time for us to pause and ask ourselves the all-important question: If I had to haul my own garbage to the landfill would I have so darn much of it?

And it rolls around just in time to remind us not to go overboard on the other major holidays we have coming up: Thanksgiving, Christmas, Black Friday and Cyber Monday. Between Thanksgiving and New Year's we toss twenty-five percent more trash than we do the rest of the year. It's all that wrapping paper, packaging and fruitcake we haul to the curb, wrenching our backs and wrecking the holiday season for trash collectors everywhere.

What follows is my Christmas gift to you and sanitation workers. It's not as much fun as a pet rock, but there's less packaging.

Five Ways to Use Less Stuff This Holiday Season

1. **Clean up your Christmas card list**. I read that there are more than a billion Christmas cards sold each year in the United States and that they'd fill a football field ten stories high. That would definitely interfere with the game.

    I'd like to tell all my family and friends across the country that the reason I've all but stopped sending Christmas cards is out of concern for their landfill—and their football stadiums—but that would be a lie. And I don't like to lie during the holiday season.

    The truth is I have good intentions, but good intentions do not send Christmas cards, at least not without assistance. On the bright side, my negligence has benefitted my community's landfill. When I don't send cards no one sends me any either.

2. **Make your own Christmas ornaments** using items you already have on hand. Not only would you be recycling, but you could also make it a fun family project. But supervise closely. When my son was in kindergarten he made an ornament by cutting his face out of his new 5x7 school portrait. He punched a hole through it and hung his creation on the tree with a bread bag tie. While I had to

admire his ingenuity, that is not what I intended for the photograph I had just paid the equivalent of a year's worth of Christmas presents for.

3. **Bring your own shopping bags.** Americans use one hundred billion plastic grocery bags every year. That's "billion" with a B. I'm trying to do my part. I use canvas bags, always remembering that the best canvas bag is the one you remember to bring to the store. I also reuse my plastic grocery bags over and over until the bottom falls out, which means I occasionally have to recycle an egg carton sooner than I intended.

4. **Reuse ribbon and wrapping paper**. Every year thirty-eight thousand miles of ribbon are used and discarded during the holidays season. That's enough ribbon to tie a bow around the earth, though I'm not sure why we would do that.

I do reuse my holiday bows. I think the fact that they're usually squashed makes me look more organized by giving the impression that I purchased and wrapped the gifts months ago and have been storing them ever since.

I read that if we all wrapped just three presents in re-used materials rather than using new paper, it would save enough paper to cover forty-five thousand football fields. What a nice gift for the football fan on your list.

And remember some gifts don't have to be wrapped at all, for example gift certificates, plants and airline tickets. I know I appreciate all of these. Or you could just give me money.

5. **Don't buy dumb gifts**. More knickknacks, gimcracks, doohickeys and thingamajigs are purchased before Christmas than any other time of the year, most of them because the giver has no other good idea. But you have options:

- **Give your time instead of buying physical gifts**. Volunteer to babysit or help a friend with home improvement projects. If I'm on your gift list—and I sincerely hope I am—you could come clean my gutters.

- **Give a donation to a favorite charity in your friend or family member's name.** Young children especially enjoy this.

- **Make gifts yourself.** Weave a rug out of some of your extra plastic bags or give away the homemade Christmas ornaments that didn't turn out so well. Homemade gifts can be wonderful. But if you're planning to give me a basket made with Popsicle sticks, I'd rather have the Popsicles.

- **Remember that old saying, it's better to regift than to receive.** Some people are offended to find out their gift is a regift though, so if you're caught it's best to be honest. Tell your recipient gently that you felt it was better to regift than to add the item to the nearly five pounds of trash you're already throwing away every day. That should make them feel better.

Cooks in Crisis

EVERY YEAR WHILE I PREPARE our Thanksgiving meal, such as it is, I tune into the annual live call-in show, *Turkey Confidential*, on National Public Radio. Food experts talk turkey about all sorts of dishes I'd love to gobble up. Don't worry. I've now used up all my turkey puns.

And on the biggest cooking day of the year, *Turkey Confidential* guests come to the rescue of cooks in crisis across America. I've always appreciated how they don't shame their callers for forgetting to thaw the turkey or using instant mashed potatoes. But I've never had the nerve to call them myself, though I've had my share of cooking crises, and not just on Thanksgiving. It may be called *Turkey Confidential* but it's on the radio, so how confidential can it be?

If I'd been able to overcome my embarrassment, there are a few calls I would have made over the many years I've listened to the show. I trust you to keep these in confidence.

1. Help! My goose is cooked but my turkey isn't. I told my guests we'd eat at noon. Then I told them one. It's now two. The relish tray is empty and someone sampled the pumpkin pie, but the turkey juices are far from clear and the little pop-up thingie shows no sign of popping up. Opening the oven every five minutes to check probably isn't helping.

   I should have seen this coming. Our turkey wasn't quite thawed even after it sat in our fridge for four days, maybe because our refrigerator runs a little cold. That usually isn't a problem since I mostly just use it to make ice cubes.

   If that weren't bad enough, our oven has been running a little cold too, maybe out of sympathy for the refrigerator. This isn't as big a problem as you'd think because I rarely use it. And a repairman told me that if I added thirty degrees to whatever temperature setting the recipe called for, I could get by for a long time, especially as little as I use my oven. But I'm beginning to wonder now if thirty degrees is enough.

   My question is, should I go ahead and serve my guests leftover tuna casserole now and have the turkey as a bedtime snack? A lot of people sleep after Thanksgiving dinner anyway.

2. How do you get rid of those little lumps in the gravy and is it absolutely necessary that you do so? In the past I've always told my guests that my gravy recipe includes little dumplings.

3. Does the five-second rule apply if you drop the turkey as you're moving it from the oven to the counter?

In case you're not familiar with it, *Turkey Confidential* people, the five-second rule is the theory that it's safe to pick up and eat food that has fallen on the floor as long as you do it within five seconds of dropping it. Silly, isn't it? I base my judgment about whether to eat what's fallen entirely on what was dropped, where it was dropped and who saw me drop it.

And I've never yet dropped a turkey. But I've lived in fear of it ever since what my family kindly refers to as the Swiss steak incident. They were all seated at the table watching me carry a steaming casserole dish heaped with Swiss steak from the kitchen to the dining room. Suddenly my elbow hit the doorway and I dropped the casserole dish. Tomato sauce sprayed our beige walls and chunks of meat and pieces of broken casserole dish flew as far as the living room. There was a collective gasp from the dinner table but I remained calm, partly because the hot tomato sauce was flying away from me. We went out to dinner after that. But have you ever tried to find an open restaurant on Thanksgiving Day?

4. I have a little problem. Actually it's a big problem. My overly enthusiastic husband bought a turkey so large it barely fits in our refrigerator. I'm not exaggerating. We had to remove the shelf above it to make room for it and that leaves very little space for anything else. We'll probably have to serve our turkey with no side dishes and no desserts. My question is, can we come to your house for Thanksgiving dinner?

Poultry in Motion and Other Questionable Thanksgiving Traditions

APPARENTLY TURKEYS AREN'T THE ONLY ONES who aren't keen on Thanksgiving. I recently stumbled on an article that listed Thanksgiving traditions the rest of the world—and even some Americans—find peculiar.

Some people interviewed for the article questioned the very motivation for the holiday. One American living in Costa Rica said her friends think it's odd that we have a celebration focused entirely on "stuffing our faces." They're missing the point. That's not what Thanksgiving is about at all. It's about getting a day off work. And napping. Oh yes, and giving thanks. And anyway we're not "stuffing our faces." We're enjoying ridiculous amounts of food in the company of people we love.

This person also said her friends wonder why there has to be a turkey involved. Well, of course there has to be a turkey. If you roast a chicken you won't have leftovers for the next two weeks.

Someone else criticized the use of marshmallows on sweet potatoes. As a marshmallow fan I don't see the harm in it. I realize it gives the dish a bit of an identity crisis. It can't decide if it's a dessert or a side dish. But that's all cleared up later when you serve the pie.

An immigrant interviewed for the article said he's been living in America for seventeen years and he still can't fathom why anyone would eat gravy. And he hasn't even had mine.

I happen to think mashed potatoes and gravy make life worth living. But I did agree with some of the criticism directed at the Thanksgiving celebration. Another immigrant talked about his family's first effort at a Thanksgiving feast. Practically in unison, all his family members spat their cranberries into their napkins. Cranberries are an acquired taste and I spent years trying to acquire it myself. I finally gave up. Now I just take extra stuffing.

One woman said that eating the Thanksgiving meal at three or four in the afternoon is no way to celebrate a holiday. I couldn't agree more. Waiting to eat forces your guests to graze all morning. And overgrazing can lead to a loss of appetite by the time the meal is served. More disciplined guests may hold off on snacking, but as the smell of roasting turkey fills the house they get hungrier and grumpier. Who wants to be grumpy on a holiday? We have the whole rest of the year for that.

Several people wondered about the presidential pardoning of turkeys, which I also find strange. Since George Washington, presidents have had the constitutional power to pardon those who've committed federal offenses. Over time they've pardoned a lot of turkeys—and not just the feathered kind.

You don't need pardoning unless you've committed a crime and it's usually pretty clear what those "turkeys" have done. But as far as we know, the only crime Tom Turkey has committed is being born a turkey and that's not a federal offense.

No one in the article mentioned what I consider the most bizarre of all Thanksgiving traditions: turkey bowling. There are variations, but basically the ball is a frozen turkey you fling toward ten large, unopened plastic soda bottles which serve as the pins.

I love to bowl. In fact for a few years whenever we spent the holiday with one branch of the family, it was our tradition to go bowling on the evening of Thanksgiving. You would think frozen turkey bowling would have been right up my...uh...alley.

But I once took part in a frozen turkey bowling fundraiser and my technique wasn't exactly poultry in motion, maybe because my heart just wasn't in it. Or maybe because I'm not that good a bowler.

But it bothers me to waste food and I doubted anyone was going to eat the turkey after twenty-five bowlers had spent the afternoon flinging it across the gym floor. On the other hand, it was nice to throw a Butterball instead of a gutter ball for a change.

What Time is Turkey Time?

LISTENING TO A COOKING SHOW on the radio one day, I heard the editor of a food magazine say that 4 p.m. is the "proper" time, indeed the *only* time, to serve Thanksgiving dinner. If your turkey is done any earlier you should toss it in the trash and start over. No, he didn't say that.

He did say that it's only logical to serve Thanksgiving dinner later in the day because, "It's dinner after all." Fair enough, except four seems a little early for dinner, especially for a stuffed shirt like him.

I'm sure he'd be appalled that I grew up eating Thanksgiving dinner at lunchtime. My mother might have preferred four. It takes a long time to cook a turkey big enough to serve a family of twelve. I think she put ours in the oven around Halloween.

I'm exaggerating. But I do recall her rising practically in the middle of the night to put a turkey the size of a yearling heifer into the oven. I don't need a bird that big so I continue to serve our Thanksgiving meal at noon or when the turkey is done, whichever comes first. And my guests have never complained—at least not about the time we ate.

I was curious about when other people serve their Thanksgiving meal so I went to that fount of all knowledge, the internet, and discovered there are more than two hundred million results on the question. I didn't read them all because there isn't time before Thanksgiving. But I did find a survey that claims more Americans serve their turkey between four and five than any other time, with those who serve it between three and four coming in a close second.

Big deal. I'm sticking with my routine. I'm a rebel and a nonconformist and I like it that way. Besides, I have some very good reasons for serving my Thanksgiving feast at noon. For one thing I have to eat every four or five hours if the people I love are going to keep loving me back.

So whether I serve my turkey at noon or not, I will need a meal at noon, and if I'm going to have a noon meal, it may as well include a turkey. I'm going to have to cook the darned thing anyway.

This means that by the time Stuffed Shirt is eating his "dinner," I'm enjoying a second piece of pie. And when he's doing his dishes, I'm having leftover turkey for supper. It's so much more efficient my way.

Besides, for most people there are basic components of Thanksgiving Day. If you leave any of them out all you have is a Thursday with extra calories. For some, it's not Thanksgiving unless there's a turkey and stuffing. For others it's a football game or the Macy's Thanksgiving Day Parade. For me it isn't Thanksgiving unless there's an afternoon nap.

As the cook, I could never nap *before* dinner—not with preparations to be made and the smell of a roasting turkey filling the house. If I don't eat until four, I'm not going to be able to fit my nap in until almost bedtime.

Most importantly though, eating at four would interfere with my all-important turkey noodle soup ritual and I refuse to do that. If it weren't for the promise of turkey noodle soup, I'd serve prime rib on Thanksgiving.

Immediately after Thanksgiving dinner/lunch, I put the turkey carcass and other magical ingredients into my stockpot. Then I let it simmer the rest of the day in preparation for National Turkey Noodle Soup Day, which is celebrated every year on the Friday after Thanksgiving—at least by me. Along with soup, the traditional Turkey Noodle Soup Day meal includes leftover pie and other desserts. And by the way, it's best served at noon.

Give Thanks
for Leftovers

IT'S ALMOST TURKEY TIME, that special time of year we set aside to focus on everything we have to be thankful for—unless we're turkeys. And some of us are.

But I don't want to talk about that now. This is a time to be happy. 'Tis the season to give thanks for our many blessings, spend quality time with our loved ones and gripe about leftovers—sometimes while spending quality time with our loved ones.

I realize there are people who gripe about leftovers year around. But almost everyone complains about them in the days after Thanksgiving. And some are still complaining for weeks after Thanksgiving. That's because despite their apparent frustration with holiday leftovers, they insist on roasting a turkey the size of Plymouth Rock. For heaven's sake, if you really don't want leftovers, stuff a Cornish game hen or roast a couple of hotdogs. You'll be loved and appreciated by turkeys everywhere.

I, however, will never give up the colossal Thanksgiving turkey. Nor will I ever complain about leftovers. I love leftovers—not eating them though. I love serving them. The benefits of serving leftovers far outweigh the benefits of cooking something new—especially if you're the one who does the cooking.

Feeding your family leftovers saves time. Not only do you spend less time grocery shopping and washing pots and pans, your family spends less time eating.

Leftovers also save money, which you can spend eating out—with or without your family.

And serving leftovers saves the whole family calories. Forget the low-carb eating plans and the low-fat diets. Try the leftover food diet. After eight or nine days of leftover turkey and stuffing, I guarantee your appetite will be depressed. I mean *suppressed*.

Those of us who are unencumbered by good taste regularly enjoy these and the many other benefits of serving leftovers: We only have to plan meals every three or four days. Our spouses are always wanting to go out to dinner. And unwelcome guests rarely return. But if they do they bring food.

That's why I was so surprised to read the following startling statistic: Despite the many benefits of leftovers, at least one hundred and forty-six million tons of food go into American landfills each year. Even more shocking, the average family wastes nearly one third of the food they buy. How can I say this nicely? If you're tossing a third of your food into the trashcan, you're not only average, you're nuts.

Think of the time, money and calories you could save if you started serving all your leftovers.

Start this Thanksgiving. If your turkey is big enough and you have plenty of freezer bags, you could serve leftovers through the Fourth of July. Now there's something to be thankful for.

Paltry Poultry

MOST THANKSGIVINGS, you'll find my husband and one of my brothers at our dinner table gnawing on turkey legs like a couple of peasants at a renaissance festival. And he never said so, but I suspected my spouse considered it a silver lining of the pandemic that he'd have both drumsticks to himself on Thanksgiving 2020.

Even though we were going to be alone for the holiday he'd been adamant that we have the whole feast, so I'd selected the smallest turkey I could find. On Thanksgiving morning he began to prepare it as he does every year. I was pondering how quiet our holiday was compared to previous years, when I heard frantic hollering from the kitchen. "There's no legs...no wings...no pop-up thing." I rushed to the kitchen to discover that someone had indeed stolen our turkey's appendages. It was barbaric.

Maybe not. A glance at the package revealed there'd been no "fowl" play after all. I hadn't purchased a small turkey. I'd brought home a large turkey breast.

My husband looked downright betrayed. I was disappointed too. We both think turkeys would be better if they were made up entirely of dark meat. We had none of that and it was my fault. I'd have been sent to my room without dinner if it wasn't my job to make everything else.

It's hard to believe it's possible, but things went downhill from there. My husband assumed that the small bag that came with our turkey contained giblets. It didn't. It was a packet of gravy and it sprayed the kitchen when he tore it open.

And he'd been right about there being no pop-up temperature indicator in our turkey breast. Of course, those are pointless if the turkey doesn't cook, but I'm getting ahead of myself.

We had to eat something so my normally mild-mannered spouse jammed the turkey breast into the oven unceremoniously and left the kitchen to grieve. I set about making the potatoes, green beans and stuffing—the boxed kind that doesn't require contact with a turkey. Good thing. We got so hungry we gobbled it up later as an appetizer.

I may have been a little preoccupied thinking about our paltry poultry because I didn't notice that something was missing in my kitchen: the aroma of roasting turkey. When I checked the turkey it was as cold as my darling's heart at the moment.

It's possible that in the confusion, I'd bumped the switch and turned the oven off. That's easy to do with our oven. But I prefer to think he forgot to turn it on in the first place because that makes us even.

How to Feel Thankful without Pumpkin Pie

DID YOU KNOW that the first harvest festival which inspired Thanksgiving actually lasted three days? That's approximately the same amount of time it takes to digest the average modern Thanksgiving dinner. And it shows that despite the many hardships they endured, even the Pilgrims were able to set aside time to celebrate, eat too much and lie on the couch watching the Macy's Thanksgiving Day Parade.

Thanksgiving continues to be a time to focus on all we have to be thankful for. It's an annual reminder that even in the most difficult of circumstances there are always reasons to be thankful—and overeat.

There are the little things—fleece, spatulas, baked goods, that little light on our dashboard that reminds us that we're about to run out of gas.

There are the big things—family, friends, the undo function on our computer.

And there are the bad things that could have been worse things. For example, I'm grateful I wasn't going very fast the day I pulled away from the gas pump with the nozzle still in my tank. And that I wasn't injured when I accidentally stepped on the gas while my arm was still in my mailbox. And that in both cases nobody was watching.

The pilgrims knew the value of gratitude and they hadn't even heard of its now well-documented social, psychological and physical benefits. I try to enjoy some of those benefits myself and not just on Thanksgiving. Each evening I do a daily accounting of a few things I'm grateful for. It's harder than you'd think. I'm tired and cranky at the end of the day and I don't have the pumpkin pie to inspire me. So I've created the following checklist to remind me of all I have to be grateful for. Try it yourself.

1. **Have I recently said to myself, "Well, that went well"?** That's exactly what I said when a highway patrol officer gave me a warning instead of a ticket. Maybe not exactly. Maybe what I really said was, "Well, that didn't go as badly as I thought it was going to go." And I had the good sense to wait to say it until the officer was back in his car and on the road.

2. **Have I said "whew" lately?** Sometimes the best thing that happened is that nothing *worse* happened. I said "whew" when my overhead door still worked after I drove into my garage a little more quickly than I should have. And when the oil in my frying pan caught fire and only destroyed my dinner and not my entire kitchen. And when I

accidentally walked into a men's restroom and no one was using it.

3. **What am I taking for granted?** I take for granted that I'll turn on the faucet and water will come out. And that I'll flip a switch and the lights will come on. Or at least I took them both for granted until a few months ago when the power went out in my neighborhood for half a day and the next day a waterline broke in front of my house. Events like these remind you to appreciate what you've been taking for granted—and to change the batteries in your flashlight.

4. **What do I just love?** I love it when I find one more pistachio in a bag I thought was empty. And I really love it when it's not one of those you need a hammer to open. I love mornings as long as they start at a reasonable hour. I love moose tracks ice cream, rare prime rib and deep-dish supreme pizza. And I love diet cola because I love balance.

5. **Is there a rose in that thorn bush?** It's easy to be grateful when I don't get a single robo call all day or when traffic lights turn green as I approach or when parking spots open up as I enter the lot. But there are days when I feel like the world is a bird-cage and I'm lining the bottom. That's when being grateful takes a bit more effort. It's still doable though, when I ask myself this insightful question.

Here's an example. I just wandered around my house for half an hour, cellphone in hand, looking for my reading glasses. And when I finally found them I realized I'd laid my phone down somewhere on my journey. So I wandered all over the house again looking for it. Where's the rose in that thorn bush? you ask. I just put four thousand steps on my Fitbit.

I'm pretty sure I hold the record for the longest time ever on hold. But on the bright side, thanks to the speaker on my phone, I was able to use the time to sort and throw in a load of laundry; make a grocery list; cook, eat, and wash the lunch dishes; move the laundry to the dryer; take a nap; play five games of solitaire, take the laundry out of the dryer and fold it all without cricking my neck.

And yes, it's true that the smoke alarm in the hallway near my kitchen is extremely sensitive. That can be very annoying and even embarrassing when we have guests. The silver lining is that every time it goes off I'm reassured that the darn thing works. I'm also thankful that there isn't a fire every time it happens. But I haven't made Thanksgiving dinner yet.

Other books by Dorothy Rosby include:

Alexa's a Spy and Other Things to Be Ticked Off About: Humorous Essays on the Hazards of Our Time
Part comical call to arms and part tongue-in-cheek tirade about the hassles of modern life.

I Used to Think I Was Not That Bad and Then I Got to Know Me Better
The book for people who read self-improvement books but never get any better. Also for the people who sincerely wish they would.

I Didn't Know You Could Make Birthday Cake from Scratch: Parenting Blunders from Cradle to Empty Nest
The little book of big parenting boo-boos.

To invite Dorothy to your book club or other event:

Dorothy Rosby
605-391-0028
www.dorothyrosby.com/contact

To follow Dorothy:
www.dorothyrosby.com
Twitter @dorothyrosby
facebook.com/rosbydorothy

Made in the USA
Middletown, DE
08 October 2022

12215936R10150